CW01303852

WOOD PELLET SMOKER AND GRILL COOKBOOK
THE MOST DELICIOUS RECIPES FOR FLAVORFUL BARBECUE

© **Copyright 2017**

All rights reserved. No part of this book may be reproduced in any form without permission in writing from the author. Reviewers may quote brief passages in reviews.

Disclaimer: No part of this publication may be reproduced or transmitted in any form or by any means, mechanical or electronic, including photocopying or recording, or by any information storage and retrieval system, or transmitted by email without permission in writing from the publisher.

While all attempts have been made to verify the information provided in this publication, neither the author nor the publisher assumes any responsibility for errors, omissions or contrary interpretations of the subject matter herein.

This book is for entertainment purposes only. The views expressed are those of the author alone, and should not be taken as expert instruction or commands. The reader is responsible for his or her own actions.

Adherence to all applicable laws and regulations, including international, federal, state and local laws governing professional licensing, business practices, advertising and all other aspects of doing business in the US, Canada, UK or any other jurisdiction is the sole responsibility of the purchaser or reader.

Neither the author nor the publisher assumes any responsibility or liability whatsoever on the behalf of the purchaser or reader of these materials. Any perceived slight of any individual or organization is purely unintentional.

Contents

Introduction 9
    Pellet smokers begin 9
    Is it a smoker or a grill? 10
    Who can benefit from pellet smokers? 10
    What makes a good pellet smoker? 11
    How long do wood pellets last in a smoker? 11
    How many pellets do pellet smokers use? 12

GRILLED CHICKEN 13
    Delicious Grilled BBQ Chicken Breasts 13
    Grilled Chicken Breast with Coriander-Lime Marinade 16
    Grilled Chicken Breast with Lemon and Honey Rub 19
    Grilled Chicken Breasts with Herbed Coffee Sauce 22
    Grilled Chicken Thighs with Red Pepper Marinade 25
    Grilled Chicken Tights in Spicy Marinade 28
    Grilled Light Turkey Burgers 31
    Grilled Turmeric Chicken Breast 34
    Mediterranean Grilled Chicken Breasts 36
    Smoked Turkey Wings in Pineapple Marinade 39

GRILLED PORK 42
    Grilled Avocado Pork Ribs 42
    Grilled Honey Garlic Pork Chops 45
    Grilled Mandarin Pork Loin with Honey-Mustard Sauce 48
    Grilled Pork Chops in Pineapple and Lemongrass Marinade .. 51
    Grilled Pork Chops Marinated with Lavender, Thyme and Plums 54
    Grilled Pork Cutlets in Citrus-Herbs Marinade 57

Grilled Pork Loin Roast with Anise-Honey-Beer Marinade 60
Smoked Hot Paprika Pork Tenderloin 63
Smoked Pork Ribs with Fresh Herbs 66
Smoked Pork Tenderloin with Mexican Pineapple Sauce 68

GRILLED BEEF 71

Grilled Almond-Crusted Beef Fillet 71
Grilled Beef Eye Fillet with Herb Rubs 74
Grilled Beef Steak with Molasses and Balsamic Vinegar 77
Grilled Beef Steak with Peanut Oil and Herbs 80
Grilled Beef Steaks with Beer-Honey Sauce 83
Grilled La Rochelle Beef Steak with Curried Pineapple 86
Grilled Veal Shoulder Roast with Fennel and Thyme Rub 89
Grilled Veal with Mustard Lemony Crust 92

GRILLED BURGERS 94

All-Time Classic Burger on Pellet Grill 94
Green Meaty Patties on Pellet Grill 97
Grilled Cheesy Turkey Patties with Pita Bread 100
Grilled Chicken Patties 103
Grilled Double Cheese Burgers 106
Grilled Lamb Burgers 109
Grilled Meatballs Stuffed with Feta Cheese 112
Mediterranean Delicious Meatballs on Pellet Grill 115
Spicy Hamburgers on Pellet Grill 118
Traditional Greek Meatballs 121

GRILLED SAUSAGES 124

Bacon Cheeseburger Sausages with Mustard 124
Easy Grilled Chicken Sausages Recipe 126
Grilled Hot Italian Sausages with Balsamic Peppers 129
Grilled Lemony Sausages 132
Grilled Sausage with Sherry Vinegar Peppers 135
Grilled Sausages with Pickled Allium 137
Grilled Vienna Sausages-New Potatoes & Snow Peas Skewers 140

- Grilled Spicy Sausages with Mustard-Caper Sauce 142
- Grilled Wrapped Bacon Sausages with Mustard Marinade 144
- Smoked Sausages with Mustard and Ketchup 147

GRILLED FISH/SEAFOOD 149
- Grilled Calamari with Mustard Oregano and Parsley Sauce 149
- Grilled Cuttlefish with Spinach and Pine Nuts Salad 152
- Grilled Dijon Lemon Catfish Fillets 155
- Grilled Halibut Fillets in Chili Rosemary Marinade 158
- Grilled Lobster with Lemon Butter and Parsley 161
- Grilled Salmon Skewers with French Antilles Sauce 164
- Grilled Salmon with Cilantro Butter 167
- Grilled Trout in White Wine and Parsley Marinade 170
- Perfect Smoked Sardine on Pellet Grill 173
- Stuffed Squid on Pellet Grill 176

GRILLED VEGETABLES 179
- Basic Grilled Garlic Eggplant 179
- Grilled Artichokes with Garlic Parsley Sauce 182
- Grilled Asparagus with Garlic and Oregano 185
- Grilled Balsamic-Honey Glazed Sweet Onions.. 188
- Smoked Potatoes with Herbs on Pellet Grill 191

GRILLED RED MEAT 194
- Grilled Goat Skewers with Lemony Herbed Marinade 194
- Grilled Greek Herb Marinated Lamb Skewers 197
- Grilled Lamb Chops with Herbed Brown Sugar Marinade 200
- Grilled Orange-Turmeric Lamb Skewers 203
- Grilled Rabbit with Wine and Rosemary Marinade 206

GRILLED GAME 209
- Grilled Wild Boar Steaks with Blueberry Sauce 209
- Grilled Wild Goose Breast in Beer Marinade 212
- Grilled Wild Rabbit with Rosemary and Garlic 215
- Smoked Aromatic Pheasant on Pellet Grill.. 218
- Stuffed Wild Duck on Pellet Grill 221

References 223

Introduction

Smoked meat is a treat fit for kings. The smoky aroma and the scented bites recall scenes of a fresh forest soaked with dew, frolicking wild game and blooming nature. There is a lot of charm not only in eating smoked meat, but making it as well.

Meat smoking is a science, art and passion rolled into one. You'll find plenty of differing opinions online and in books on how to smoke meat the right way, but what's important is what fits you. Meat needs to be smoked with pleasure because only then will it be eaten with pleasure.

Meat has to be prepared before smoking and each type of meat takes a different approach. Some of these tips and tricks can be given through books and in person, but everything else must be learned first-hand. So keep going steady, don't give up, and relish the journey as much as the destination.

As you journey through the smoky valley of delight, remember to share everything you've learned with others who are just starting their adventure. As sweet as smoked meat is, the sweetest thing is having that little bit of secret knowledge that will give it just the right kind of texture, aroma, and taste.

Pellet smokers begin

Just like stoves, pellet smokers have a thermostat that makes use a breeze. After setting a temperature on a pellet smoker, put the cut of meat inside it, close it up and walk away. When the smoking completes, you'll have the perfect cut of smoked meat, just the way you intended.

There are plenty of pellet smoker designs out there, and all of them have a bit higher price point than one could expect. Even the entry level pellet smokers can have a price tag that raises an eyebrow. This is true as long as you compare pellet smokers to grills, which is like comparing heaven and earth. For smoked meat, pellet smokers are hands down the best choice, so if you want the best results, that's what you're meant to get instead of a bullet and offset smokers.

The invention of pellet smokers came after a series of flukes. The sawmills produced plenty of sawdust that was discarded as waste until an Oregon heating company got the idea of compressing it into wood pellets to be used for their heating furnaces. In 1982, the demand for furnaces dropped off, leaving the company with a massive stockpile. The employees got together and turned furnaces into pellet grills and smokers, which then became company's official products.

These pellet smokers had a knob with three settings – low, medium, high – but no heat sensor in the oven. So, they worked as a proof of concept but not very precisely or reliably – if the outside temperature dropped rapidly but you weren't there to turn up the heat, the meat would never get smoked. Once the competitors got the gist of the idea, the pellet smokers got imbued with digital thermostats and heat sensors and the game was on. Today's models automatically feed pellets whenever the temperature drops below what you set it to.

Is it a smoker or a grill?

Despite their awesomeness, smokers still can't grill meat, at least not the way specialized grills can. Even when a smoker is advertised as a smoker-grill combo, it's likely the emphasis is on the smoking part and the steak just won't get seared the way it's meant to. The workaround is to buy a griddle, heat the smoker as high as it gets and slap the steak on the oiled griddle for some searing action.

Both smokers and grills resemble the primordial fire pit with a container for fuel below the food. The difference between the two is that grilled foods have to necessarily be exposed to air in order to turn them and add more fuel, while smokers are designed to keep everything sealed tight. Smokers also use wood instead of coal and benefit from having water (or sand) that helps keep the fire going without your intervention.

Inside a smoker, the temperature can range from 160-250 degrees F while a grill can have anywhere up to 400 F. Knowing which areas are hot and which are warm is essential to using a grill properly. Meats need to be seared by placing them on the grill area with high heat until they develop a succulent crust, and then moved to a grill area with low heat so they're cooked through. Having a much more consistent, albeit lower, temperature, smokers can have the meat thoroughly smoked without any intervention on your part. Better yet, different kinds of wood used for fuel suffuse the meat with a specific scent that's a delight in its own right.

Who can benefit from pellet smokers?

Smoked meat is the next step in enjoying barbecued meats. There are some tradeoffs, but the benefits are in getting consistently amazing flavored meats that keep and travel well. Smoking was actually the way our ancestors kept meat throughout winter, though such meats were heavily salted to prolong their shelf life. As a result, there was a tough outer crust that could pretty much chip a tooth and it would only get tougher with time. This is why cowboys used to put pieces of jerky beneath their saddles in hopes long riding sessions would make them at least remotely edible (the jerky, not the saddles).

Of course, there is a certain amount of showmanship involved with preparing a BBQ, which is just a meat party. The grill needs to be wheeled into place, which gives you the chance to take off your shirt and show those bulging pecs. BBQ can't happen without meat, which demonstrates your hunting prowess and provider ability. The fire needs to be started as well, which is another caveman task that brings out the cavewoman in nearby ladies.

All of this comes before we've done any cooking whatsoever. Once the fire under the grill is started, everything needs to move at blazing speed or things fall apart and the guests start getting cranky. If your BBQ guests pull out emergency potato chips and candy, it's over. A great BBQ primarily relies on impeccable timing to grill and serve the meat in just the right way.

After you've struggled with the logistics of preparing a BBQ, it's time to take things easy and just enjoy the moment. In short, pellet smokers benefit those who enjoy the taste of barbecue but want to avoid the immense amount of work involved or simply don't have the need to show off to anyone.

What makes a good pellet smoker?

Every pellet smoker has a certain set of qualities that make it good for one thing in particular. Some of them are cheap, others are compact and others yet have a great capacity. Here's the tricky part – a compact smoker might have a too steep price. Now what? A good smoker is the one that does exactly what you want it to. This means having the ability to make rich-tasting smoked meat while being the most convenient for your needs, without regards for the price.

Low-cost smokers are bound to be made out of inferior materials and not last as long as a high-quality smoker. Paying 200 bucks more for a better smoker might mean avoiding all sorts of headaches if things start going south, and get you an amazing product that will last for decades.

Pay attention to the ranges of temperature the smoker can maintain. Again, there's a lot of flexibility in this field, so define your needs beforehand. As mentioned previously, grilling needs about 400 F heat and a griddle, smoking is from 160 F and up and searing takes at least 500 F. Pay attention to the thermometer of a smoker you're eyeing and try to gauge if it can keep up the pace with your BBQ and smoking needs.

Temperature control on the smoker can come in several varieties: 1-position, 3-position, and multi-position. Anything that has a "high" position can be used for grilling and searing. Digital and programmable displays also help immensely.

Portability is the next area of interest. If you plan on smoking and grilling things at home, you can take a bulkier model since it won't be moving as much. Otherwise, if you want to adventure out to the middle of nowhere with your trusty smoker, you'd want something with less moving parts that can withstand the rough treatment.

Finally, you want to account for the smoker brand's gimmick. Some have a Wi-Fi, others come with cooking rack attachments and so on. These are mostly displayed front and center on the advertising material in order to attract the customers, but will it make a difference? You want to make sure you're not overpaying for the gimmick you'll never use.

How long do wood pellets last in a smoker?

The good news is that, by using a low temperature, a typical smoker won't be using that much fuel per hour. The bad news is that grilling eats through a bag of pellets like crazy and the pellet brand makes a huge difference. If possible, join a pellet smoker community and buy pellets in bulk to save on quantity and shipping.

You should find the pellet consumption rate in the manual or on the manufacturer's page, but on average you can go with 1-3 lbs. an hour. It is needed one pound of pellets for low temperature, two pounds of pellets for medium and three for high. Depending on what you want to do with the smoker, a 20-lb. bag of pellets will last you 10-20 hours. Something to consider is whether the smoker has inbuilt insulation, which keeps the heat inside.

Welding and heating blankets help slow down the pellet consumption a lot since they stop the heat from being drained into the atmosphere by the cold weather. Some manufacturers produce specially crafted heating blankets for your smoker, so check out how convenient it is for you. It might seem strange that you'll have to tuck in your smoker with its blanket in cold weather, but it really works.

No matter what, you'll simply have to have a stash of pellets for your smoker, so better get used to the additional cost. The wisest solution is maintaining a stash of pellets in case the price temporarily spikes for whatever reason. Also, you might want to try out different pellet flavors until you find the one that works with everything you're making with your smoker and just use that one. For example, a veteran smoker could recommend hickory, but that's entirely up to you.

How many pellets do pellet smokers use?

Now we're treading into the murky waters of pellet science. There are so many different variables a pellet brand can have, for example, an oak pellet is much denser than an Alder pellet and has a 35% higher BTU (British thermal unit), producing that much more heat as it burns up. Then there are different BTU ratings between different oak pellet brands, which again factor into the price.

Try not to panic if a pellet smoker seems to be eating the pellets at an alarming rate, especially during overnight smoking. Try to see what happens over a longer period and see if there's any difference due to lower wind speeds or better insulation before asking for advice or thinking something's wrong with your smoker.

Some pellet manufacturers produce fluffier pellets than others, which you can figure out if the pellet bag seems to have plenty of dust remaining at the bottom. In other cases, you'll encounter a debate about using heating pellets for smoking. This is not a good idea since heating pellets can be made from rotting or infested wood dragged out of swamps. When used in a heating furnace, the pellets combust completely, so there's no health danger, but if burned at typically low temperatures in a smoker, your meat can get infused with all sorts of bad bacteria. On the other hand, smoker pellets are specifically made from food-grade wood that's also used in construction.

In the next chapter, we prepared for you a cookbook with 80 versatile and very delicious recipes for your Pellet Smoker/Grill. We hope you'll enjoy!

GRILLED CHICKEN
Delicious Grilled BBQ Chicken Breasts

Ingredients

4 chicken breasts

1/4 cup Olive oil

2 clove garlic minced

1 cup BBQ sauce

1/2 cup BBQ hot sauce

2 tbsp Worcestershire sauce

Instructions

1. In a deep container place the chicken breasts.
2. In a separate bowl, combine olive oil, garlic, BBQ sauces and Worcestershire sauce.
3. Cover the chicken breasts evenly with BBQ sauce.
4. Start pellet grill on, lid open, until the fire is established (4-5 minutes). Increase the temperature to 350F and allow to pre-heat, lid closed, for 10 - 15 minutes.
5. Remove the chicken breast from the sauce (reserve sauce) and place chicken breasts direct on the hot grill and cook 15 - 20 minutes, depending on breast size (or to taste).
6. Ten minutes before the chicken is done, sprinkle on your BBQ sauce mixture.
7. Serve hot.

Servings: 6

Cooking Times

Total Time: 45 minutes

Nutrition Facts

Serving size: 1/6 of a recipe (10 ounces)

Percent daily values based on the Reference Daily Intake (RDI) for a 2000 calorie diet.

Nutrition information calculated from recipe ingredients.

Amount Per Serving

Calories 390,19

Calories From Fat (31%) 122,2

% Daily Value

Total Fat 13,71g 21%

Saturated Fat 2,2g 11%

Cholesterol 103,67mg 35%

Sodium 1423,04mg 59%

Potassium 705,01mg 20%

Total Carbohydrates 27,92g 9%

Fiber 1,2g 5%

Sugar 20,98g

Protein 35,34g 71%

Grilled Chicken Breast with Coriander-Lime Marinade

Ingredients

4 chicken fillets

1/2 cup chopped coriander

1/2 cup lime juice (3-4 limes)

1 cup of honey

4 cloves of garlic minced

2 tbsp olive oil

Salt and pepper

Instructions

1. Place your chicken breast in a "zip" freezer bag.
2. In a bowl, combine coriander, lime juice, honey, garlic, olive oil and salt and pepper.
3. Pour the coriander-lime mixture in a bag with chicken.
4. Marinate in refrigerator for 4 - 5 hours.
5. Remove the chicken from the bag and par dry on paper towel.
6. Start pellet grill on, lid open, until the fire is established (4-5 minutes). Increase the temperature to 350F and allow to pre-heat, lid closed, for 10 - 15 minutes.
7. Arrange chicken breasts on the hot grill and cook 10 - 20 minutes, depending on breast size.
8. Five minutes before ready, splash the marinade over the chicken.
9. Serve hot.

Servings: 6

Cooking Times

Inactive Time: 5 hours

Total Time: 45 minutes

Nutrition Facts

Serving size: 1/6 of a recipe (9 ounces)

Percent daily values based on the Reference Daily Intake (RDI) for a 2000 calorie diet.

Nutrition information calculated from recipe ingredients.

Amount Per Serving

Calories 440,85

Calories From Fat (32%) 140,63

% Daily Value

Total Fat 16,22g 25%

Saturated Fat 1,94g 10%

Cholesterol 100,69mg 34%

Sodium 199,48mg 8%

Potassium 1171,87mg 33%

Total Carbohydrates 49,22g 16%

Fiber 18,15g 73%

Sugar 23,56g

Protein 39g 78%

Grilled Chicken Breast with Lemon and Honey Rub

Ingredients

4 chicken breasts

3 tbsp of fresh butter

1/2 cup chicken broth

Juice of 1 lemon

1 tbsp of honey

1 clove of crushed garlic

Fresh rosemary chopped to taste

Salt and pepper

Instructions

1. In a pan melt the butter and sauté the chicken breasts for 2-3 minutes on each side until they get good color.
2. Remove from heat and let rest for 5 -10 minutes.
3. In a small bowl, stir the broth, lemon juice, honey, garlic, rosemary and salt, and pepper.
4. Rub the chicken breast generously with lemon/honey mixture.
5. Start pellet grill on, lid open, until the fire is established (4-5 minutes). Increase the temperature to 350F and allow to pre-heat, lid closed, for 10 - 15 minutes.
6. Place chicken breasts on the hot grill and cook 10 – 20 minutes, depending on breast size.
7. Serve hot.

Servings: 5

Cooking Times

Total Time: 55 minutes

Nutrition Facts

Serving size: 1/5 of a recipe (8 ounces)

Percent daily values based on the Reference Daily Intake (RDI) for a 2000 calorie diet.

Nutrition information calculated from recipe ingredients.

Amount Per Serving

Calories 293,82

Calories From Fat (36%) 106,19

% Daily Value

Total Fat 11,94g 18%

Saturated Fat 5,49g 27%

Cholesterol 139,15mg 46%

Sodium 293,66mg 12%

Potassium 725,83mg 21%

Total Carbohydrates 3,76g 1%

Fiber 0,02g <1%

Sugar 3,53g

Protein 40,69g 81%

Grilled Chicken Breasts with Herbed Coffee Sauce

Ingredients

4 boneless skinless chicken breast halves

2 tbsp melted butter or olive oil

1/4 cup packed dark brown sugar

1/2 cup chicken broth

4 slices lemon (1/4 inch thick)

1 tsp black peppercorns

1 tsp mustard seeds

1 tsp coriander seeds

3/4 cup strong brewed coffee

Salt to taste

Instructions

1. Brush your chicken breast with oil and sprinkle with salt.
2. In a large container combine all remaining ingredients and submerge your chicken breast.
3. Cover and refrigerate for 2 hours.
4. Start pellet grill on, lid open, until the fire is established (4-5 minutes). Increase the temperature to 350F and allow to pre-heat, lid closed, for 10 - 15 minutes.
5. Grill chicken, without turning, 10 minutes for boneless chicken and 10 to 15 minutes for bone-in (or to taste).
6. Serve hot.

Servings: 4

Cooking Times

Inactive Time: 2 hours

Total Time: 40 minutes

Nutrition Facts

Serving size: 1/4 of a recipe (9 ounces)

Percent daily values based on the Reference Daily Intake (RDI) for a 2000 calorie diet.

Nutrition information calculated from recipe ingredients.

Amount Per Serving

Calories 277,11

Calories From Fat (33%) 92,38

% Daily Value

Total Fat 10,38g 16%

Saturated Fat 1,89g 9%

Cholesterol 73,1mg 24%

Sodium 161,45mg 7%

Potassium 369,8mg 11%

Total Carbohydrates 18,7g 6%

Fiber 0,83g 3%

Sugar 14,92g

Protein 27,77g 56%

Grilled Chicken Thighs with Red Pepper Marinade

Ingredients

2 lb chicken thighs

1/2 cup chicken broth

1 tsp red pepper flakes

1 tsp sweet paprika

1 tsp freshly ground black pepper

1 tsp dried oregano

1 tsp curry powder

1 tbsp garlic powder

2 tbsp olive oil

Instructions

1. Place the chicken thighs in a large flat dish so they are in a single layer.
2. In a bowl, combine broth, red pepper flakes, paprika, black pepper, oregano, curry and garlic powder and olive oil.
3. Pour the mixture over chicken thighs.
4. Cover and refrigerate for 4 hours.
5. Start pellet grill on, lid open, until the fire is established (4-5 minutes). Increase the temperature to 450F and allow to pre-heat, lid closed, for 10 - 15 minutes.
6. Remove chicken tights from marinade and pat dry.
7. Place marinated chicken thighs on the grill grate, skin side down. Cook for 10 minutes, flip, and cook another 10 minutes.
8. Serve hot.

Servings: 6

Cooking Times

Inactive Time: 4 hours

Total Time: 45 minutes

Nutrition Facts

Serving size: 1/6 of a recipe (7 ounces)

Percent daily values based on the Reference Daily Intake (RDI) for a 2000 calorie diet.

Nutrition information calculated from recipe ingredients.

Amount Per Serving

Calories 230,18

Calories From Fat (41%) 94,08

% Daily Value

Total Fat 10,64g 16%

Saturated Fat 5,49g 27%

Cholesterol 125,5mg 42%

Sodium 192,51mg 8%

Potassium 398,7mg 11%

Total Carbohydrates 1,84g <1%

Fiber 0,45g 2%

Sugar 0,12g

Protein 30,48g 61%

Grilled Chicken Tights in Spicy Marinade

Ingredients

6 chicken tights

2 cloves garlic minced

1/3 cup balsamic vinegar

1/3 cup olive oil

2 tbsp mustard

Salt and ground pepper

1 tbsp oregano

1 tsp coriander

1 tbsp BBQ dry spice mix

Instructions

1. Place the chicken tights in a shallow dish in a single layer.
2. In a bowl, combine the garlic, balsamic vinegar, oil, mustard, salt and pepper, oregano coriander and BBQ dry spice mix.
3. Pour the mixture over chicken thighs evenly.
4. Marinate in refrigerator for 4 hours.
5. Start pellet grill on, lid open, until the fire is established (4-5 minutes). Increase the temperature to 350F and allow to pre-heat, lid closed, for 10 - 15 minutes.
6. Remove the chicken tights from marinade and par dry on kitchen towel.
7. Place marinated chicken thighs on the grill grate, skin side down. Cook for 10 minutes, flip, and cook another 10 minutes.
8. Serve hot.

Servings: 6

Cooking Times

Inactive Time: 4 hours

Total Time: 45 minutes

Nutrition Facts

Serving size: 1/6 of a recipe (7.5 ounces)

Percent daily values based on the Reference Daily Intake (RDI) for a 2000 calorie diet.

Nutrition information calculated from recipe ingredients.

Amount Per Serving

Calories 438,7

Calories From Fat (66%) 291,34

% Daily Value

Total Fat 32,54g 50%

Saturated Fat 7,38g 37%

Cholesterol 138,61mg 46%

Sodium 195,02mg 8%

Potassium 371,1mg 11%

Total Carbohydrates 3,7g 1%

Fiber 0,64g 3%

Sugar 2,2g

Protein 30,78g 62%

Grilled Light Turkey Burgers

Ingredients

2 lbs ground turkey

1 small red bell pepper

1 onion finely chopped

1/2 bunch fresh chopped parsley

1 large egg

Salt and pepper to taste

1/2 tsp dry thyme

1/2 tsp dry oregano

Instructions

1. Place the ground turkey meat along with all remaining ingredients in a deep ball.
2. Using your hands, knead the mixture well.
3. Wet your hands with water and make patties.
4. Start pellet grill on, lid open, until the fire is established (4-5 minutes). Increase the temperature to 350F and allow to pre-heat, lid closed, for 10 - 15 minutes.
5. Place the turkey burgers on the grill and cook for 5 - 7 minutes, covered, until nice grill marks form. Flip and continue to cook, covered, for 3-5 minutes more.
6. The internal temperature for food safety for ground turkey as recommended by the USDA is 165°F.
7. Serve hot.

Servings: 6

Cooking Times

Total Time: 40 minutes

Nutrition Facts

Serving size: 1/6 of a recipe (8 ounces)

Percent daily values based on the Reference Daily Intake (RDI) for a 2000 calorie diet.

Nutrition information calculated from recipe ingredients.

Amount Per Serving

Calories 252,06

Calories From Fat (45%) 112,63

% Daily Value

Total Fat 12,48g 19%

Saturated Fat 3,34g 17%

Cholesterol 135,33mg 45%

Sodium 101,51mg 4%

Potassium 454,13mg 13%

Total Carbohydrates 3,59g 1%

Fiber 0,96g 4%

Sugar 1,92g

Protein 31,26g 63%

Grilled Turmeric Chicken Breast

Ingredients

4 chicken breasts, boneless, skinless

4 cloves garlic, finely diced

1/2 cup chicken fat

1 tsp turmeric powder, or to taste

Table salt to taste

Instructions

1. Take a boneless, skinless chicken breast and cut it lengthwise into pieces.
2. Combine the chicken fat, turmeric, diced garlic and rub evenly the chicken breast.
3. Start pellet grill on, lid open, until the fire is established (4-5 minutes). Increase the temperature to 350F and allow to pre-heat, lid closed, for 10 - 15 minutes.
4. Place chicken breasts on the hot grill and cook 10 - 15 minutes, depending on breast size.
5. Serve hot.

Servings: 4

Cooking Times

Total Time: 45 minutes

Nutrition Facts

Serving size: 1/4 of a recipe (9 ounces)

Percent daily values based on the Reference Daily Intake (RDI) for a 2000 calorie diet.

Nutrition information calculated from recipe ingredients.

Amount Per Serving

Calories 477,14

Calories From Fat (57%) 285,88

% Daily Value

Total Fat 31,7g 49%

Saturated Fat 8,98g 45%

Cholesterol 172,82mg 58%

Sodium 274,27mg 11%

Potassium 885,23mg 25%

Total Carbohydrates 0,99g <1%

Fiber 0,06g <1%

Sugar 0,03g

Protein 50,29g 101%

Mediterranean Grilled Chicken Breasts

Ingredients

4 chicken breasts

Marinade

1/4 cup olive oil

1/2 cup white wine

1 lemon zest

1 small onion chopped

3 cloves of garlic minced

1 tsp oregano

1 tsp rosemary chopped

Salt and pepper to taste

Lemon slices for garnish

Instructions

1. Place a chicken breast in a large container.
2. In a bowl, combine all ingredients together for marinade and pour over chicken.
3. Refrigerate for 2 - 3 hours.
4. Start pellet grill on, lid open, until the fire is established (4-5 minutes). Increase the temperature to 350F and allow to pre-heat, lid closed, for 10 - 15 minutes.
5. Remove chicken breast from marinade and pat dry on a kitchen towel.
6. Arrange chicken breasts on the hot grill and cook 10 -15 minutes, depending on breast size (or to taste).
7. Let rest 10 minutes before slicing. Serve with lemon slices.

Servings: 6

Cooking Times

Inactive Time: 3 hours

Total Time: 6 minutes

Nutrition Facts

Serving size: 1/6 of a recipe (8 ounces)

Percent daily values based on the Reference Daily Intake (RDI) for a 2000 calorie diet.

Nutrition information calculated from recipe ingredients.

Amount Per Serving

Calories 286,72

Calories From Fat (41%) 116,71

% Daily Value

Total Fat 13,12g 20%

Saturated Fat 2,15g 11%

Cholesterol 100,69mg 34%

Sodium 184,89mg 8%

Potassium 637,48mg 18%

Total Carbohydrates 3,27g 1%

Fiber 0,61g 2%

Sugar 1,12g

Protein 33,78g 68%

Smoked Turkey Wings in Pineapple Marinade

Ingredients

2 lbs turkey wings cut at joint

1 can (11 oz) tomato sauce

1 can (11 oz) pineapple with juice

1 tbsp brown sugar firmly packed

2 tsp chili powder

1/4 tsp ground ginger

1/4 tsp garlic powder

Salt and pepper

Instructions

1. Place the turkey wings in a wide dish in a single layer.
2. In a bowl, combine tomato sauce, pineapple, brown sugar, chili powder, ginger, garlic powder and salt and pepper.
3. Pour the pineapple mixture over the turkey wings.
4. Marinate in refrigerator for 4 - 5 hours.
5. Remove the turkey wings from marinade and pat dry with kitchen towel.
6. Place the turkey wing sections on the hot side of the grill and cook for approximately 5 minutes per side until browned and then move to the cool side of the grill.
7. Cover the grill and allow wings to smoke for approximately 40 minutes more until cooked through (at least 165 °F internal temperature) and tender.
8. Serve hot.

Servings: 6

Cooking Times

Inactive Time: 5 hours

Total Time: 1 hour and 15 minutes

Nutrition Facts

Serving size: 1/6 of a recipe (6,3 ounces).

Percent daily values based on the Reference Daily Intake (RDI) for a 2000 calorie diet.

Nutrition information calculated from recipe ingredients.

Amount Per Serving

Calories 107,12

Calories From Fat (14%) 14,99

% Daily Value

Total Fat 1,69g 3%

Saturated Fat 0,41g 2%

Cholesterol 7,7mg 3%

Sodium 393,87mg 16%

Potassium 398,77mg 11%

Total Carbohydrates 21,45g 7%

Fiber 2,15g 9%

Sugar 18,96g

Protein 3,7g 7%

GRILLED PORK
Grilled Avocado Pork Ribs

Ingredients

2 lbs spare ribs

1 cup avocado oil

1 tsp garlic salt, or to taste

1 tsp garlic powder

1/2 tsp onion powder

Salt and pepper, to taste

Instructions

1. In a bowl, combine avocado oil, garlic salt, garlic powder, onion powder, and salt and pepper.
2. Place the pork chops in a shallow container and pour avocado mixture evenly over.
3. Cover and refrigerate for at least 4 hours, or overnight.
4. Start pellet grill on, lid open, until the fire is established (4-5 minutes). Increase the temperature to 450F and allow to pre-heat, lid closed, for 10 - 15 minutes.
5. Arrange pork chops on the grill and cook about 4 - 5 minutes. Flip and cook on the other side for another 4 minutes.
6. Transfer pork chops on serving plate and serve hot with French fries and salad.

Servings: 6

Cooking Times

Total Time: 45 minutes

Nutrition Facts

Serving size: 1/6 of a recipe (6.5 ounces)

Percent daily values based on the Reference Daily Intake (RDI) for a 2000 calorie diet.

Nutrition information calculated from recipe ingredients.

Amount Per Serving

Calories 512,48

Calories From Fat (82%) 439,63

% Daily Value

Total Fat 53,55g 82%

Saturated Fat 13,49g 67%

Cholesterol 120,96mg 40%

Sodium 464,59mg 19%

Potassium 374,04mg 11%

Total Carbohydrates 0,7g <1%

Fiber 0,25g 1%

Sugar 0,03g

Protein 23,5g 47%

Grilled Honey Garlic Pork Chops

Ingredients

1/4 cup honey

1/4 cup lemon juice freshly squeezed

1 tbsp dry sherry

2 tbsp tamari sauce

2 cloves garlic, minced

Salt and pepper to taste

4 boneless center-cut lean pork chops (about 5 ounces each)

Instructions

1. Combine honey, lemon juice, sherry, tamari sauce, garlic and salt and pepper in a bowl.
2. Place pork in a container and pour marinade over pork.
3. Cover and marinate in a fridge overnight.
4. Remove pork from marinade and pat dry with kitchen paper towel (reserve marinade for later).
5. Start your pellet on Smoke with the lid open until the fire is established (4 - 5 minutes). Increase temperature to 450F and preheat, lid closed, for 10 - 15 minutes.
6. Arrange the pork chops on the grill and cook about 10 minutes. Flip and grill on the other side for another 8 minutes.
7. In a meantime, heat remaining marinade in small saucepan over medium heat to simmer.
8. Transfer pork chops on a serving plate, pour with marinade and serve hot.

Servings: 4

Cooking Times

Total Time: 55 minutes

Nutrition Facts

Serving size: 1/4 of a recipe (8 ounces)

Percent daily values based on the Reference Daily Intake (RDI) for a 2000 calorie diet.

Nutrition information calculated from recipe ingredients.

Amount Per Serving

Calories 296,59

Calories From Fat (18%) 53,11

% Daily Value

Total Fat 5,87g 9%

Saturated Fat 2,06g 10%

Cholesterol 112,27mg 37%

Sodium 587,57mg 24%

Potassium 713,39mg 20%

Total Carbohydrates 19,8g 7%

Fiber 0,19g <1%

Sugar 17,95g

Protein 39,29g 79%

Grilled Mandarin Pork Loin with Honey-Mustard Sauce

Ingredients

4 lbs pork loin

Mandarin Habanero Seasoning Rub

Sauce

1 cup honey

1 cup mustard

1 cup tangerine juice

1 tbsp garlic powder

1 tsp white pepper

Instructions

1. Start pellet grill on, lid open, until the fire is established (4 - 5 minutes). Increase the temperature to 375F and allow to pre-heat, lid closed, for 10 - 15 minutes.
2. Generously rub the pork loin with Mandarin Habanero Seasoning Rub.
3. In a saucepan whisk all ingredients for the sauce over medium heat, about 4 - 5 minutes.
4. Place the pork on hot grill and cook for 35 minutes at 375 degrees.
5. After 15 minutes pour with honey/mustard sauce and continue to grill.
6. When the meat reaches an internal temperature around 140 degrees pull it off, cover it and let it rest for 5 to 10 minutes
7. Slice and serve hot.

Servings: 8

Cooking Times

Total Time: 1 hour and 25 minutes

Nutrition Facts

Serving size: 1/8 of a recipe (11 ounces)

Percent daily values based on the Reference Daily Intake (RDI) for a 2000 calorie diet.

Nutrition information calculated from recipe ingredients.

Amount Per Serving

Calories 434,62

Calories From Fat (17%) 75,68

% Daily Value

Total Fat 8,4g 13%

Saturated Fat 2,78g 14%

Cholesterol 149,69mg 50%

Sodium 290,27mg 12%

Potassium 949,43mg 27%

Total Carbohydrates 37,41g 12%

Fiber 0,72g 3%

Sugar 35,73g

Protein 51,87g 104%

Grilled Pork Chops in Pineapple and Lemongrass Marinade

Ingredients

1/4 cup canned pineapple juice

4 tbsp lemongrass

1/2 cup fresh cilantro, chopped

3 tbsp fresh mint

2 tbsp minced fresh ginger

2 tbsp minced garlic

2 tsp grated lime zest

1/2 cup chicken broth

4 pork chops

Lime wedges for serving

Ingredients

1. In a bowl, combine pineapple juice, lemongrass, cilantro, mint, ginger, garlic, chicken broth and lime zest.
2. Put the chops in a large zip-top bag and pour in the marinade.
3. Seal the bag and refrigerate overnight.
4. Start your grill on Smoke with the lid open until the fire is established (4 - 5 minutes). Set the temperature to 450F (or High) and preheat, lid closed, for 10 to 15 minutes.
5. Remove the pork chops from the marinade and drain off and discard the liquid.
6. Place on the grill and cook until the pork chop releases from the grill, about 4 minutes. Flip and cook on the other side for another 3 minutes.
7. Cover the grill and cook the chops indirectly until their internal temperature reaches 145° to 150°F, another 3 to 5 minutes per side.
8. Transfer pork chops to serving plate and serve.

Servings: 4

Cooking Times

Total Time: 45 minutes

Nutrition Facts

Serving size: 1/4 of a recipe (9 ounces)

Percent daily values based on the Reference Daily Intake (RDI) for a 2000 calorie diet.

Nutrition information calculated from recipe ingredients.

Amount Per Serving

Calories 242

Calories From Fat (23%) 55,54

% Daily Value

Total Fat 6,14g 9%

Saturated Fat 2,13g 11%

Cholesterol 112,27mg 37%

Sodium 182,26mg 8%

Potassium 798,91mg 23%

Total Carbohydrates 4,86g 2%

Fiber 1,16g 5%

Sugar 1,21g

Protein 39,58g 79%

Grilled Pork Chops Marinated with Lavender, Thyme and Plums

Ingredients

2 tbsp olive oil

3 tsp cooking dry lavender

2 tsp light brown sugar

2 tsp fresh thyme, chopped

Salt and grated black pepper

2 cloves of garlic, finely chopped

4 pork chops or fillets

1/4 cup honey

2 tsp balsamic vinegar

4 ripe plums

Instructions

1. In a bowl, combine oil, lavender, sugar, thyme, salt, pepper and garlic and stir well.
2. Place the pork chops in a container and pour with the oil-lavender mixture.
3. Marinate at room temperature for 30 minutes.
4. Meanwhile, in a pan, pour the honey and balsamic vinegar and cook over moderate to low heat until boil. Stir until all the ingredients are combined well. Set aside.
5. Start pellet grill on, lid open, until the fire is established (4-5 minutes). Increase the temperature to 225 and allow to pre-heat, lid closed, for 10 - 15 minutes.
6. Remove chops from marinade and pat dry with kitchen towel.
7. Arrange pork chops on grill and cook until the pork chop releases from the grill, about 5 minutes. Flip and cook on the other side for another 4 minutes.
8. Put the plums, cut into the middle, on the grill and bake until golden, about 2 minutes.
9. Brush the plums on both sides with the honey sauce and let them cook for about another minute.
10. Pour the honey sauce over pork chops, and serve with grilled plums.

Servings: 4

Cooking Times

Total Time: 1 hour and 5 minutes

Nutrition Facts

Serving size: 1/4 of a recipe (7 ounces)

Percent daily values based on the Reference Daily Intake (RDI) for a 2000 calorie diet.

Nutrition information calculated from recipe ingredients.

Amount Per Serving

Calories 287,76

Calories From Fat (31%) 90,52

% Daily Value

Total Fat 10,17g 16%

Saturated Fat 2,09g 10%

Cholesterol 61,38mg 20%

Sodium 48,44mg 2%

Potassium 492,34mg 14%

Total Carbohydrates 28,64g 10%

Fiber 1,26g 5%

Sugar 26,59g

Protein 21,54g 43%

Grilled Pork Cutlets in Citrus-Herbs Marinade

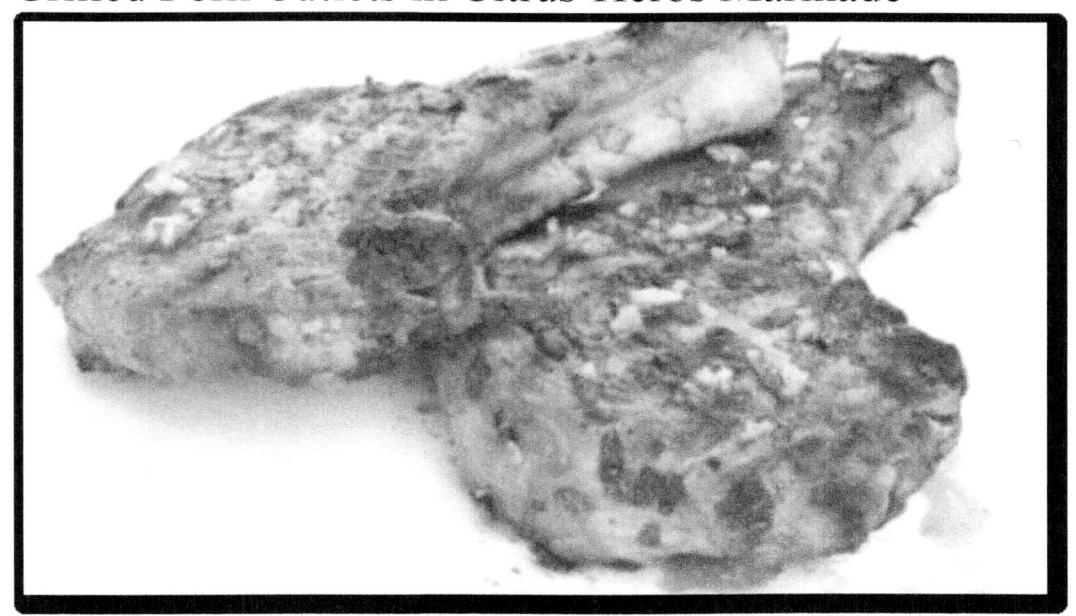

Ingredients

4 pork cutlets

2 large lemons freshly squeezed

1 orange juice

10 twigs of coriander

2 tbsp of fresh parsley, finely chopped

1 tsp of ground caraway

1 clove of garlic minced

2 tbsp of olive oil

Salt and ground black pepper

Instructions

1. Place the pork cutlets in a large resealable bag along with lemon juice, orange juice, coriander, parsley, caraway, minced garlic, olive oil and salt and pepper.
2. Refrigerate at least 4 hours, or overnight.
3. When ready, remove the pork cutlets from marinade and pat dry with kitchen towel.
4. Start pellet grill on, lid open, until the fire is established (4-5 minutes). Increase the temperature to 450F and allow to pre-heat, lid closed, for 10 - 15 minutes.
5. Place pork chops on the grill grate and cook for 10 minutes per side (or to taste).
6. Serve hot.

Servings: 4

Cooking Times

Total Time: 45 minutes

Nutrition Facts

Serving size: 1/4 of a recipe (8 ounces)

Percent daily values based on the Reference Daily Intake (RDI) for a 2000 calorie diet.

Nutrition information calculated from recipe ingredients.

Amount Per Serving

Calories 259,42

Calories From Fat (41%) 105,31

% Daily Value

Total Fat 11,81g 18%

Saturated Fat 2,67g 13%

Cholesterol 93,56mg 31%

Sodium 71,38mg 3%

Potassium 642,72mg 18%

Total Carbohydrates 4,91g 2%

Fiber 0,41g 2%

Sugar 2,58g

Protein 32,23g 64%

Grilled Pork Loin Roast with Anise-Honey-Beer Marinade

Ingredients

MARINADE

1 red onion finely diced

1/4 cup honey

1 cup dark beer

1 tsp Anise seeds

3 tbsp mustard

1 tbsp fresh thyme, finely chopped

Salt and pepper

PORK

3 lbs pork loin

Instructions

1. Combine all ingredients for the marinade in a bowl.
2. Place the pork along with marinade mixture in a resealable plastic bag.
3. Refrigerate for several hours, or overnight.
4. On the next day, remove the pork from marinade (reserve marinade for later) and place on kitchen towel.
5. Prepare the grill on Smoke with the lid open until the fire is established (4 to 5 minutes). Set the temperature to 350F and preheat, lid closed, for 10 to 15 minutes.
6. Place the pork on grill rack and cook uncovered for 1 hour.
7. Pour the reserved marinade over the pork and continue to roast for 45 minutes.
8. Your meat is ready when the internal temperature of the pork is 165F.
9. Remove the meat from the grill and let rest for 10 minutes before slicing.
10. Serve hot or cold.

Servings: 6

Cooking Times

Total Time: 2 hours and 20 minutes

Nutrition Facts

Serving size: 1/6 of a recipe (11 ounces)

Percent daily values based on the Reference Daily Intake (RDI) for a 2000 calorie diet.

Nutrition information calculated from recipe ingredients.

Amount Per Serving

Calories 404,56

Calories From Fat (25%) 101,55

% Daily Value

Total Fat 11,34g 17%

Saturated Fat 3,8g 19%

Cholesterol 149,69mg 50%

Sodium 246,81mg 10%

Potassium 932,68mg 27%

Total Carbohydrates 18,61g 6%

Fiber 0,76g 3%

Sugar 11,68g

Protein 52,15g 104%

Smoked Hot Paprika Pork Tenderloin

Ingredients

2 lb pork tenderloin

3/4 cup chicken stock

1/2 cup tomato-basil sauce

2 tbsp smoked hot paprika (or to taste)

1 tbsp oregano

Salt and pepper to taste

Instructions

1. In a bowl, combine the chicken stock, tomato-basil sauce, paprika, oregano, salt, and pepper together.
2. Brush generously over the outside of the tenderloin.
3. Start the pellet grill on Smoke with the lid open until the fire is established (4 to 5 minutes). Set the temperature to 225F and preheat, lid closed, for 10 to 15 minutes.
4. Place the pork on the grill grate and smoke until the internal temperature of the pork is at least medium-rare (about 145F), for 2-1/2 to 3 hours.
5. Before slicing let rest for 10 minutes.
6. Serve.

Servings: 6

Cooking Times

Total Time: 3 hours and 35 minutes

Nutrition Facts

Serving size: 1/6 of a recipe (8 ounces)

Percent daily values based on the Reference Daily Intake (RDI) for a 2000 calorie diet.

Nutrition information calculated from recipe ingredients.

Amount Per Serving

Calories 360,71

Calories From Fat (36%) 129,21

% Daily Value

Total Fat 14,32g 22%

Saturated Fat 5,1g 26%

Cholesterol 159,8mg 53%

Sodium 331,83mg 14%

Potassium 905,83mg 26%

Total Carbohydrates 3,21g 1%

Fiber 1,46g 6%

Sugar 1,01g

Protein 52,09g 104%

Smoked Pork Ribs with Fresh Herbs

Ingredients

1/4 cup olive oil

1 tbsp garlic minced

1 tbsp crushed fennel seeds

1 tsp fresh parsley, finely chopped

1 tsp fresh sage, finely chopped

1 tsp fresh rosemary, finely chopped

Salt and ground black pepper to taste

3 lbs. bone-in pork rib roast

Instructions

1. Combine the olive oil, garlic, fennel seeds, parsley, sage, rosemary, salt, and pepper in a bowl; stir well.
2. Coat each chop on both sides with the herb mixture.
3. Start the pellet grill on SMOKE with the lid open until the fire is established (4 to 5 minutes).
4. Smoke the ribs for 3 hours.
5. Transfer the chops to a serving platter and serve hot.

Servings: 6

Cooking Times

Total Time: 3 hours and 20 minutes

Nutrition Facts

Serving size: 1/6 of a recipe (8 ounces)

Percent daily values based on the Reference Daily Intake (RDI) for a 2000 calorie diet.

Nutrition information calculated from recipe ingredients.

Amount Per Serving

Calories 458,73

Calories From Fat (61%) 280,34

% Daily Value

Total Fat 31,29g 48%

Saturated Fat 6g 30%

Cholesterol 116,2mg 39%

Sodium 113,68mg 5%

Potassium 701,82mg 20%

Total Carbohydrates 1,19g <1%

Fiber 0,49g 2%

Sugar 0,02g

Protein 40,92g 82%

Smoked Pork Tenderloin with Mexican Pineapple Sauce

Ingredients

Pineapple Sauce

1 can (11 oz) unsweetened crushed pineapple

1 can (11 oz) roasted tomato or tomatillo

1/2 cup port wine

1/4 cup orange juice

1/4 cup packed brown sugar

1/4 cup lime juice

2 tbsp Worcestershire sauce

1 tsp garlic powder

1/4 tsp cayenne pepper

PORK

2 pork tenderloin (1 pound each)

1 tsp ground cumin

1/2 tsp pepper

1/4 tsp cayenne pepper

2 tbsp lime juice (freshly squeezed)

Instructions

1. Combine cumin, pepper, cayenne pepper and lime juice and rub over tenderloins.
2. Start the pellet grill on Smoke with the lid open until the fire is established (4 to 5 minutes). Set the temperature to 225F and preheat, lid closed, for 10 to 15 minutes.
3. Arrange the tenderloin on the grill grate and smoke until the internal temperature of the pork is at least 145F (medium-rare), 2-1/2 to 3 hours.
4. Let rest for 5 minutes before slicing.

FOR SAUCE

1. In a saucepan, combine the sauce ingredients. Bring to a boil; cook 20-25 minutes or until mixture is reduced by half, stirring occasionally.
2. Remove from heat and let cool.
3. Serve pork slices with pineapple sauce and lime wedges.

Servings: 6

Cooking Times

Total Time: 3 hours and 55 minutes

Nutrition Facts

Serving size: 1/6 of a recipe (10 ounces)

Percent daily values based on the Reference Daily Intake (RDI) for a 2000 calorie diet.

Nutrition information calculated from recipe ingredients.

Amount Per Serving

Calories 277,85

Calories From Fat (11%) 31,32

% Daily Value

Total Fat 3,49g 5%

Saturated Fat 1,08g 5%

Cholesterol 98,28mg 33%

Sodium 248,93mg 10%

Potassium 825,47mg 24%

Total Carbohydrates 24,31g 8%

Fiber 0,67g 3%

Sugar 18,13g

Protein 32,42g 65%

GRILLED BEEF
Grilled Almond-Crusted Beef Fillet

Ingredients

3 lbs. fillet of beef tenderloin

Salt and pepper to taste

1/4 cup olive oil

1/3 cup onion, very finely chopped

2 tbsp curry powder

1 cup chicken broth

1 tbsp Dijon mustard

1/4 cup sliced almonds, coarsely chopped

Instructions

1. Rub the beef tenderloin with salt and pepper.
2. In a bowl, combine olive oil, onion, curry, chicken broth, mustard, and almonds.
3. Rub your beef meat generously with the curry mixture.
4. Start your pellet grill, set the temperature on High and preheat, lid closed, for 10 to 15 minutes.
5. As a general rule, you should grill steaks on high heat (450-500°F).
6. Grill about 7-10 minutes per side at high temperatures or 15-20 minutes per side at the lower temperatures, or to your preference for doneness.
7. Remove meat from the grill and let cool for 10 minutes.
8. Serve hot.

Servings: 4

Cooking Times

Total Time: 55 minutes

Nutrition Facts

Serving size: 1/4 of a recipe (9 ounces)

Percent daily values based on the Reference Daily Intake (RDI) for a 2000 calorie diet.

Nutrition information calculated from recipe ingredients.

Amount Per Serving

Calories 479,33

Calories From Fat (65%) 309,35

% Daily Value

Total Fat 34,54g 53%

Saturated Fat 12,82g 64%

Cholesterol 145,22mg 48%

Sodium 358,36mg 15%

Potassium 669,63mg 19%

Total Carbohydrates 4,05g 1%

Fiber 1,95g 8%

Sugar 0,7g

Protein 36,82g 74%

Grilled Beef Eye Fillet with Herb Rubs

Ingredients

2 lbs. beef eye fillet

Salt and pepper to taste

2 tbsp Olive oil

1/4 cup parsley, fresh and chopped

1/4 cup oregano leaves, fresh and chopped

2 tbsp basil, fresh and chopped

2 tbsp rosemary leaves, fresh and chopped

3 cloves garlic, crushed

Instructions

1. Season beef roast with salt and pepper and place in a shallow dish.
2. In a medium bowl, combine olive oil, chopped parsley, basil, oregano, rosemary, garlic, and oil. Rub the meat with the herb mixture from both sides
3. Bring the meat to room temperature 30 minutes before you put it on the grill.
4. Start your pellet grill, set the temperature on High and preheat, lid closed, for 10 to 15 minutes.
5. As a general rule, you should grill steaks on high heat (450-500°F).
6. Grill about 7-10 minutes per side at high temperatures or 15-20 minutes per side at the lower temperatures, or to your preference for doneness.
7. When ready, let meat rest for 10 minutes, slice and serve.

Servings: 6

Cooking Times

Total Time: 8 hours

Nutrition Facts

Serving size: 1/6 of a recipe (6.5 ounces)

Percent daily values based on the Reference Daily Intake (RDI) for a 2000 calorie diet.

Nutrition information calculated from recipe ingredients.

Amount Per Serving

Calories 427,93

Calories From Fat (67%) 285,93

% Daily Value

Total Fat 31,8g 49%

Saturated Fat 11,63g 58%

Cholesterol 128,52mg 43%

Sodium 79,46mg 3%

Potassium 563,23mg 16%

Total Carbohydrates 3,78g 1%

Fiber 2,17g 9%

Sugar 0,2g

Protein 30,8g 62%

Grilled Beef Steak with Molasses and Balsamic Vinegar

Ingredients

2 1/2 lbs beefsteak grass fed

Salt and ground pepper

2 tbsp molasses

1 cup beef broth

1 tbsp red wine vinegar

1 tbsp balsamic vinegar

Instructions

1. Place a beef steak in a large dish.
2. Combine the beef broth, molasses, red wine vinegar and balsamic vinegar in a bowl.
3. Cover, and refrigerate for up to 8 hours.
4. 30 minutes before grilling, remove the steaks from the refrigerator and let sit at room temperature.
5. Start your pellet grill, set the temperature on High and preheat, lid closed, for 10 to 15 minutes.
6. Grill about 7-10 minutes per side at high temperatures or 15-20 minutes per side at the lower temperatures.
7. Transfer meat to a serving dish and let rest about 10 minutes.
8. Serve warm.

Servings: 5

Cooking Times

Inactive Time: 8 hours

Total Time: 50 minutes

Nutrition Facts

Serving size: 1/5 of a recipe (10 ounces)

Percent daily values based on the Reference Daily Intake (RDI) for a 2000 calorie diet.

Nutrition information calculated from recipe ingredients.

Amount Per Serving

Calories 295,3

Calories From Fat (19%) 56,21

% Daily Value

Total Fat 6,21g 10%

Saturated Fat 2,39g 12%

Cholesterol 124,74mg 42%

Sodium 307,23mg 13%

Potassium 923,44mg 26%

Total Carbohydrates 6,55g 2%

Fiber 0g 0%

Sugar 4,92g

Protein 52,89g 106%

Grilled Beef Steak with Peanut Oil and Herbs

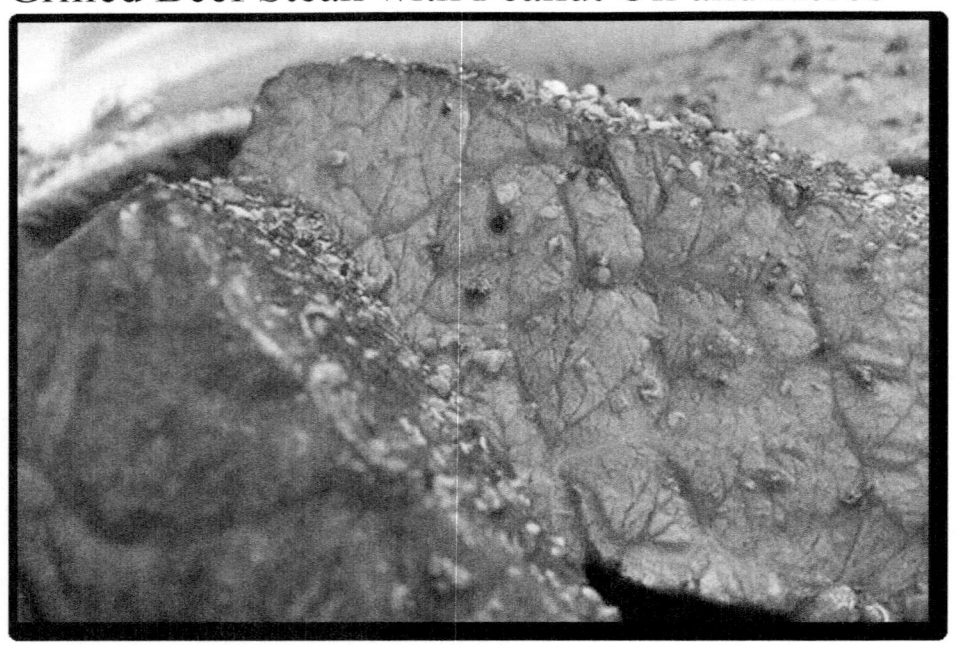

Ingredients

3 lbs beef steak, preferably flank

1 tsp sea salt

2 tbsp peanut oil

1/4 olive oil

2 tbsp fresh mint leaves, finely chopped

2 tsp peppercorn black

2 tsp peppercorn green

1/2 tsp cumin seeds

1 pinch of chili flakes

Instructions

1. Rub the beef steaks with coarse salt and place in a large dish.
2. Make a marinade; in a bowl, combine peanut oil, olive oil, fresh mint leave, peppercorn, cumin and chili flakes.
3. Cover and refrigerate for 4 hours.
4. Bring the meat to room temperature 30 minutes before you put it on the grill.
5. Start your pellet grill, set the temperature on High and preheat, lid closed, for 10 to 15 minutes.
6. As a general rule, you should grill steaks on high heat (450-500°F).
7. Grill about 7-10 minutes per side at high temperatures or 15-20 minutes per side at the lower temperatures, or to your preference for doneness.
8. Remove flank steak from the grill and let cool before slicing for 10 -15 minutes.
9. Slice and serve.

Servings: 6

Cooking Times

Inactive Time: 4 hours and 45 minutes

Total Time: 55 minutes

Nutrition Facts

Serving size: 1/6 of a recipe (9 ounces)

Percent daily values based on the Reference Daily Intake (RDI) for a 2000 calorie diet.

Nutrition information calculated from recipe ingredients.

Amount Per Serving

Calories 346,3

Calories From Fat (39%) 135,16

% Daily Value

Total Fat 15,15g 23%

Saturated Fat 3,73g 19%

Cholesterol 124,74mg 42%

Sodium 246,8mg 10%

Potassium 781,86mg 22%

Total Carbohydrates 0,21g <1%

Fiber 0,07g <1%

Sugar 0g

Protein 32,38g 75%

Grilled Beef Steaks with Beer-Honey Sauce

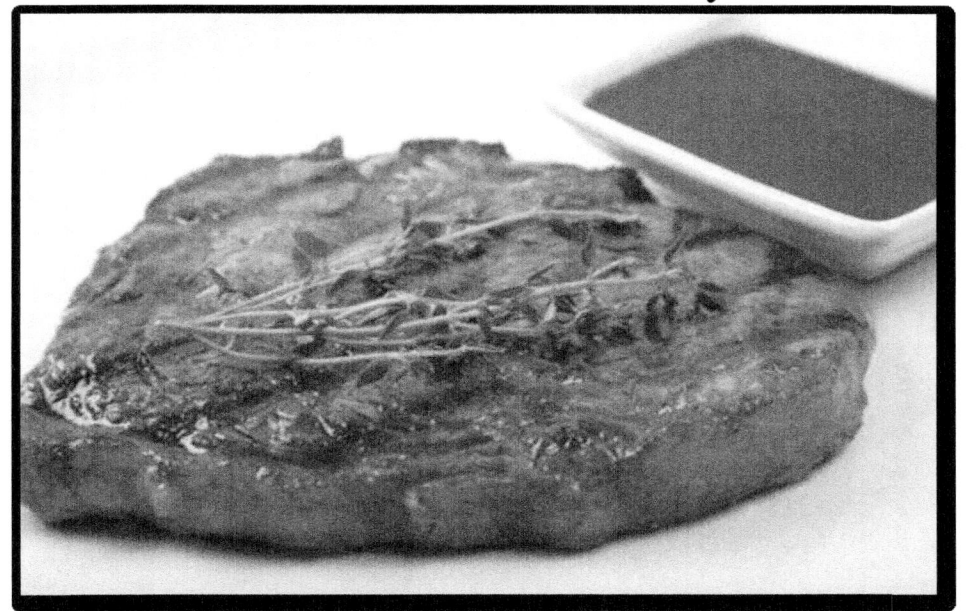

Ingredients

4 beef steaks

Salt and pepper to taste

1 cup of beer

1 tsp thyme

1 tbsp of honey

1 lemon juice

2 tbsp olive oil

Instructions

1. Season beef steaks with salt and pepper.
2. In a bowl, combine beer, thyme, honey, lemon juice and olive oil.
3. Rub the beef steaks generously with beer mixture.
4. Start your pellet grill, set the temperature on High and preheat, lid closed, for 10 to 15 minutes.
5. As a general rule, you should grill steaks on high heat (450-500°F).
6. Grill about 7-10 minutes per side at high temperatures or 15 minutes per side at the lower temperatures, or to your preference for doneness.
7. Remove meat from the grill and let cool for 10 minutes.
8. Serve.

Servings: 4

Cooking Times

Total Time: 55 minutes

Nutrition Facts

Serving size: 1/4 of a recipe (11 ounces)

Percent daily values based on the Reference Daily Intake (RDI) for a 2000 calorie diet.

Nutrition information calculated from recipe ingredients.

Amount Per Serving

Calories 355,77

Calories From Fat (32%) 112,22

% Daily Value

Total Fat 12,57g 19%

Saturated Fat 3,16g 16%

Cholesterol 117,7mg 39%

Sodium 120,76mg 5%

Potassium 768,79mg 22%

Total Carbohydrates 7,68g 3%

Fiber 0,18g <1%

Sugar 4,69g

Protein 49,74g 99%

Grilled La Rochelle Beef Steak with Curried Pineapple

Ingredients

1 1/2 lbs flank steak

1/4 cup olive oil

8 oz pineapple chunks in juice

3 tsp curry powder

1 tbsp red currant jelly

1/2 tsp salt, or to taste

Instructions

1. Place the flank steak in a shallow dish.
2. In a bowl, combine olive oil, pineapple chunks in juice, curry powder, red currant jelly and salt and pepper.
3. Pour the mixture over flank steak.
4. Cover and refrigerate for 4 hours.
5. Bring the meat to room temperature 30 minutes before you put it on the grill.
6. Start your pellet grill, set the temperature on High and preheat, lid closed, for 10 to 15 minutes.
7. As a general rule, you should grill steaks on high heat (450-500°F).
8. Grill about 7-10 minutes per side at high temperatures or 15-20 minutes per side at the lower temperatures, or to your preference for doneness.
9. Remove flank steak from the grill and let cool for 10 minutes.
10. Serve hot.

Servings: 4

Cooking Times

Inactive Time: 4 hours and 30 minutes

Total Time: 55 minutes

Nutrition Facts

Serving size: 1/4 of a recipe (8 ounces)

Percent daily values based on the Reference Daily Intake (RDI) for a 2000 calorie diet.

Nutrition information calculated from recipe ingredients.

Amount Per Serving

Calories 406,26

Calories From Fat (57%) 232,53

% Daily Value

Total Fat 26,1g 40%

Saturated Fat 7,03g 35%

Cholesterol 101,21mg 34%

Sodium 372,67mg 16%

Potassium 584,26mg 17%

Total Carbohydrates 10,41g 3%

Fiber 1,85g 7%

Sugar 8,23g

Protein 32,01g 64%

Grilled Veal Shoulder Roast with Fennel and Thyme Rub

Ingredients

3 1/2 lb boneless veal shoulder roast

2 tbsp dried thyme leaves

1 fresh fennel, thinly sliced

2 tbsp fresh thyme, chopped

3/4 tsp kosher salt and ground white pepper

4 tbsp olive oil

1/2 cup white wine

Instructions

1. Place a shoulder roast in a large dish and rub with salt and pepper.
2. In a bowl, combine thyme, fennel, salt and pepper, wine and oil.
3. Rub the meat generously.
4. Start your pellet grill, set the temperature on High and preheat, lid closed, for 10 to 15 minutes.
5. Grill about 25 minutes at high temperatures or to your preference for doneness.
6. Remove the veal chops from the grill. Take their temperature with your meat thermometer. The veal chops should have a temperature of 130 degrees Fahrenheit for medium-rare or 140 degrees for medium.
7. Serve hot.

Servings: 8

Cooking Times

Total Time: 55 minutes

Nutrition Facts

Serving size: 1/8 of a recipe (10 ounces)

Percent daily values based on the Reference Daily Intake (RDI) for a 2000 calorie diet.

Nutrition information calculated from recipe ingredients.

Amount Per Serving

Calories 322,71

Calories From Fat (33%) 108,01

% Daily Value

Total Fat 12,14g 19%

Saturated Fat 2,97g 15%

Cholesterol 132,68mg 44%

Sodium 126,25mg 5%

Potassium 799,83mg 23%

Total Carbohydrates 4,64g 2%

Fiber 1,39g 6%

Sugar 0,62g

Protein 36,23g 72%

Grilled Veal with Mustard Lemony Crust

Ingredients

1 lb boneless veal leg round roast

1 tbsp Dijon-style mustard

1 tbsp lemon juice

1 tsp dried thyme, crushed

1 tsp dried basil, crushed

2 tbsp water

1/2 tsp coarsely salt and ground pepper

1/4 cup breadcrumbs

Instructions

1. Place meat on a rack in a shallow roasting pan.
2. In a small mixing bowl stir together bread crumbs, water, mustard, lemon juice, basil, thyme, and pepper. Spread the mixture over surface of the meat.
3. Start your pellet grill, set the temperature on High and preheat, lid closed, for 10 to 15 minutes.
4. As a general rule, you should grill steaks on high heat (450-500°F).
5. Grill about 7-10 minutes per side at high temperatures or 15-20 minutes per side at the lower temperatures, or to your preference for doneness.
6. Remove veal meat from the grill and let cool for 10 minutes.

Servings: 8

Cooking Times

Total Time: 2 hours and 45 minutes

Nutrition Facts

Serving size: 1/8 of a recipe

Percent daily values based on the Reference Daily Intake (RDI) for a 2000 calorie diet.

Nutrition information calculated from recipe ingredients.

Amount Per Serving

Calories 172

Calories From Fat (17%) 28,49

% Daily Value

Total Fat 3g 5%

Saturated Fat 1g 5%

Cholesterol 108mg 36%

Sodium 218mg 9%

Total Carbohydrates 4g 1%

Fiber 0g 0%

Protein 30g 60%

GRILLED BURGERS
All-Time Classic Burger on Pellet Grill

Ingredients

1 1/4 lbs ground beef

1/2 lb ground pork

1 onion, finely chopped

1 tbsp fresh parsley, finely chopped

Salt and freshly ground black pepper, to taste

1/4 cup olive oil

Mayonnaise, mustard or ketchup for garnish

Instructions

1. Combine all ingredients from the list in a large bowl.
2. Using your hands, knead well. Form into 6 round patties.
3. Place patties in the refrigerator for 30 minutes.
4. Start the pellet grill on high with the lid open until the fire is established. Set the temperature to 425F and preheat, lid closed, for 10 to 15 minutes.
5. Place patties on grill rack and grill the burgers for 3 to 4 minutes on each side.
6. Serve hot with mayonnaise, mustard or ketchup.

Servings: 6

Cooking Times

Inactive Time: 30 minutes

Total Time: 30 minutes

Nutrition Facts

Serving size: 1/6 of a recipe (6.5 ounces)

Percent daily values based on the Reference Daily Intake (RDI) for a 2000 calorie diet.

Nutrition information calculated from recipe ingredients.

Amount Per Serving

Calories 436,68

Calories From Fat (76%) 332,67

% Daily Value

Total Fat 36,57g 56%

Saturated Fat 12,08g 60%

Cholesterol 98,09mg 33%

Sodium 87,49mg 4%

Potassium 386,14mg 11%

Total Carbohydrates 1,92g <1%

Fiber 0,35g 1%

Sugar 0,87g

Protein 23,33g 47%

Green Meaty Patties on Pellet Grill

Ingredients

2 green onions, finely chopped

1 lb frozen spinach, thawed and drained

2 lb minced beef meat

3 cloves garlic

1 egg

3 tbsp olive oil

1 tbsp fresh tarragon and cilantro, finely chopped

Salt and ground pepper to taste

Instructions

1. Wash the green onions and chop finely. Place the onion in a deep bowl, and add spinach; stir well.
2. Add the ground meat, garlic, egg, oil, tarragon and cilantro and pepper and salt to taste. Knead until all ingredients are combined well.
3. Using your hands, knead the meat mixture well and shape 6 patties.
4. Start your pellet grill on high with the lid open until the fire is established. Set the temperature to 380F and preheat, lid closed, for 10 to 15 minutes.
5. Arrange patties on grill rack and cook 4 - 5 minutes per side.
6. Serve hot.

Servings: 6

Cooking Times

Total Time: 35 minutes

Nutrition Facts

Serving size: 1/6 of a recipe (10 ounces)

Percent daily values based on the Reference Daily Intake (RDI) for a 2000 calorie diet.

Nutrition information calculated from recipe ingredients.

Amount Per Serving

Calories 456,88

Calories From Fat (66%) 302,29

% Daily Value

Total Fat 32,76g 50%

Saturated Fat 12,87g 64%

Cholesterol 144,4mg 48%

Sodium 375,76mg 16%

Potassium 709,91mg 20%

Total Carbohydrates 8,36g 3%

Fiber 3,59g 14%

Sugar 2,42g

Protein 31,42g 63%

Grilled Cheesy Turkey Patties with Pita Bread

Ingredients

1 lb ground turkey breast, raw

1 tsp dried oregano, crushed

Salt and black pepper to taste

2 tsp green onions, finely chopped

Chili peppers

1/4 cup light cream cheese

1/4 cup shredded Cheddar cheese

1 tomato

1 cucumber

1/2 avocado

2 wheat pita bread rounds, halved crosswise

Instructions

1. In a bowl, combine ground turkey meat, salt, pepper, and the oregano.
2. Using your hands, knead the meat and form the meat into 4 patties.
3. Start your pellet grill on SMOKE with the lid open until the fire is established. Set the temperature to 380F and preheat, lid closed, for 10 to 15 minutes.
4. Cook the burgers until golden brown and slightly charred on the first side, about 5 - 6 minutes.
5. Meanwhile, in a small bowl, combine the chopped green onion, chili pepper, cream cheese, cheddar cheese and salt to taste.
6. Open cut sides of pita bread and spread cream cheese mixture inside. Add grilled turkey patties, avocado, tomato and cucumber slices. Serve.

Servings: 4

Cooking Times

Total Time: 25 minutes

Nutrition Facts

Serving size: 1/4 of a recipe (10 ounces)

Percent daily values based on the Reference Daily Intake (RDI) for a 2000 calorie diet.

Nutrition information calculated from recipe ingredients.

Amount Per Serving

Calories 251,33

Calories From Fat (26%) 64,31

% Daily Value

Total Fat 7,44g 11%

Saturated Fat 1,98g 10%

Cholesterol 56,21mg 19%

Sodium 1132,54mg 40%

Potassium 742,73mg 21%

Total Carbohydrates 19,64g 7%

Fiber 4,21g 17%

Sugar 7,55g

Protein 26,94g 54%

Grilled Chicken Patties

Ingredients

2/3 cup minced onion

2 lb ground chicken breast

2 tbsp fresh parsley, finely chopped

1 tbsp cilantro (chopped)

2 tbsp olive oil

1/8 tsp crushed red pepper flakes, or to taste

1/2 tsp ground cumin

2 tbsp fresh lemon juice

3/4 tsp kosher salt

2 tsp paprika

Hamburger buns for serving

Instructions

1. Clean and chop the onions as finely as you can.
2. Place onion in a deep bowl and add all ingredients from the list.
3. Using your hands, mix well. Form into 6 patties. Refrigerate until ready to grill (about 20 minutes).
4. Start your pellet grill with the lid open until the fire is established. Set the temperature to 350F and preheat, lid closed, for 10 to 15 minutes.
5. Arrange chicken patties on grill rack and cook for 10 minutes turning once.
6. Serve hot with hamburger buns and your favorite condiments.

Servings: 6

Cooking Times

Total Time: 45 minutes

Nutrition Facts

Serving size: 1/6 of a recipe (7 ounces)

Percent daily values based on the Reference Daily Intake (RDI) for a 2000 calorie diet.

Nutrition information calculated from recipe ingredients.

Amount Per Serving

Calories 223,41

Calories From Fat (34%) 76,53

% Daily Value

Total Fat 8,59g 13%

Saturated Fat 1,51g 8%

Cholesterol 96,77mg 32%

Sodium 412,49mg 17%

Potassium 615,51mg 18%

Total Carbohydrates 2,54g <1%

Fiber 0,63g 3%

Sugar 0,97g

Protein 32,47g 65%

Grilled Double Cheese Burgers

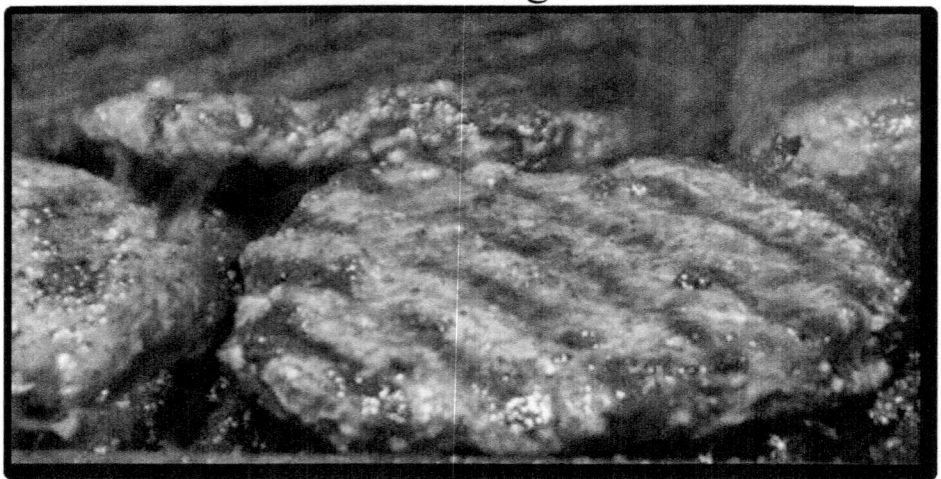

Ingredients

1 lb ground beef

2 small onions, chopped

1 cup grated Cheddar cheese

4 oz Gruyere cheese

1 egg

1 tsp nutmeg

1 tsp allspice

Sea salt and freshly black pepper to taste

Instructions

1. In a food processor, mince the Gruyere cheese. Set aside.
2. Whisk egg with grated cheddar cheese in a bowl. Add the spices, nutmeg salt, and pepper and stir well.
3. Add in chopped onions and Gruyere cheese.
4. Add the beef meet and using your hands, mix well. Form into 6 patties. Taste and adjust a salt and pepper. Refrigerate the meat mixture until ready to grill.
5. Start the pellet grill with the lid open until the fire is established (4 to 5 minutes). Set the temperature to 425F and preheat, lid closed, for 10 to 15 minutes.
6. Place patties on grill rack and cook for 4 – 5 minutes per side.
7. Serve hot.

Servings: 6

Cooking Times

Total Time: 35 minutes

Nutrition Facts

Serving size: 1/6 of a recipe (6 ounces)

Percent daily values based on the Reference Daily Intake (RDI) for a 2000 calorie diet.

Nutrition information calculated from recipe ingredients.

Amount Per Serving

Calories 384,51

Calories From Fat (68%) 262,06

% Daily Value

Total Fat 28,97g 45%

Saturated Fat 14,21g 71%

Cholesterol 128,27mg 43%

Sodium 246,39mg 10%

Potassium 306,67mg 9%

Total Carbohydrates 4,58g 2%

Fiber 0,84g 3%

Sugar 2,03g

Protein 25,23g 50%

Grilled Lamb Burgers

Ingredients

1 3/4 lbs. ground lamb

1/2 cup breadcrumbs, soaked

1 tsp dried oregano

1 large egg at room temperature

3 cloves garlic, minced

1 tbsp cumin

1 tbsp chopped fresh rosemary

1 piece cayenne pepper (more or less to taste)

Sea salt to taste

Instructions

1. In a bowl, mix ground lamb, soaked breadcrumbs, oregano, egg, garlic, cumin, rosemary, cayenne and salt until combined well.
2. Wet your hands and form the meat into 4 - 6 patties.
3. Start your pellet grill with the lid open until the fire is established. Set the temperature to 380F and preheat, lid closed, for 10 to 15 minutes.
4. Arrange lamb patties on grill rack and cook until they are beginning to firm and are hot and slightly pink in the center, about 5 - 7 minutes per side for medium-rare (or your desired degree of doneness).
5. Transfer lamb burgers to serving plate and let rest for 10 minutes.
6. Serve.

Servings: 6

Cooking Times

Total Time: 45 minutes

Nutrition Facts

Serving size: 1/6 of a recipe (8 ounces)

Percent daily values based on the Reference Daily Intake (RDI) for a 2000 calorie diet.

Nutrition information calculated from recipe ingredients.

Amount Per Serving

Calories 287,06

Calories From Fat (31%) 88,68

% Daily Value

Total Fat 9,83g 15%

Saturated Fat 3,74g 19%

Cholesterol 118,54mg 40%

Sodium 186,49mg 8%

Potassium 680,03mg 19%

Total Carbohydrates 7,65g 3%

Fiber 0,69g 3%

Sugar 0,61g

Protein 39,35g 79%

Grilled Meatballs Stuffed with Feta Cheese

Ingredients

2 lb ground beef or mixed - beef and pork

Zest of 1 lemon

1 tbsp olive oil

2 tsp oregano, fresh chopped

1/2 tsp thyme

Salt and ground pepper to taste

3/4 cup Feta cheese

Olive oil for brushing

Instructions

1. In a large bowl combine ground meat, lemon zest, olive oil, oregano, thyme and salt and pepper to taste.
2. Using your heads knead the meat mixture well.
3. Cut Feta into small cubes and start making the meatballs.
4. Take about half a tablespoon of minced meat, roll in the shape of a circle, press in the middle with your thumb, place a piece of cheese there, "close" and gently roll into balls.
5. Start your pellet grill with the lid open until the fire is established. Set the temperature to 380F and preheat, lid closed, for 10 to 15 minutes.
6. Brush meatballs with olive oil and place on grill and cook until well browned, about 8 - 10 minutes total time.
7. Serve hot.

Servings: 6

Cooking Times

Total Time: 35 minutes

Nutrition Facts

Serving size: 1/6 of a recipe (6 ounces)

Percent daily values based on the Reference Daily Intake (RDI) for a 2000 calorie diet.

Nutrition information calculated from recipe ingredients.

Amount Per Serving

Calories 430,53

Calories From Fat (73%) 315,97

% Daily Value

Total Fat 34,29g 53%

Saturated Fat 13,42g 67%

Cholesterol 116,55mg 39%

Sodium 144,17mg 6%

Potassium 405,7mg 12%

Total Carbohydrates 0,72g <1%

Fiber 0,36g 1%

Sugar 0,21g

Protein 27,32g 55%

Mediterranean Delicious Meatballs on Pellet Grill

Ingredients

2 1/2 lb ground beef

1 1/2 tbsp fresh parsley, finely chopped

1 tbsp fresh basil, finely chopped

1/2 tsp cumin

1 slice of bread, soaked

1 onion, finely chopped

2 eggs

2 tbsp olive oil

1 tsp vinegar

Salt and pepper to taste

Instructions

1. In a large bowl, mix all ingredients from the list.
2. Using clean hands, knead the ground meat mixture.
3. Wet your hands with water, and then form the meat into 12 meatballs.
4. Start your pellet grill on SMOKE with the lid open until the fire is established. Set the temperature to 380F and preheat, lid closed, for 10 to 15 minutes.
5. Arrange the patties on the grill rack and cook, turning on all sides, for about 8 minutes. (You can also thread the meatballs onto metal skewers.) Remove meatballs to a platter and let rest for 5 minutes.
6. Serve hot with your favorite condiments and salad.

Servings: 6

Cooking Times

Total Time: 40 minutes

Nutrition Facts

Serving size: 1/6 of a recipe (9 ounces)

Percent daily values based on the Reference Daily Intake (RDI) for a 2000 calorie diet.

Nutrition information calculated from recipe ingredients.

Amount Per Serving

Calories 483,02

Calories From Fat (72%) 317,3

% Daily Value

Total Fat 45,36g 70%

Saturated Fat 16,89g 84%

Cholesterol 203,75mg 68%

Sodium 177,13mg 7%

Potassium 560,78mg 16%

Total Carbohydrates 4,33g 1%

Fiber 0,5g 2%

Sugar 1,12g

Protein 36,14g 72%

Spicy Hamburgers on Pellet Grill

Ingredients

2 lbs. ground beef

1 large egg at room temperature

2 tsp chili flakes

2 tsp chili powder

30 g finely ground oats

Sea salt to taste

Lemon juice for serving

Instructions

1. Mix all ingredients from the list in a large bowl.
2. Using your hands, knead the ground meat mixture until combined well.
3. Wet your hands with water, and then form the meat into 6 patties.
4. Refrigerate them for 30 minutes.
5. Start your pellet grill with the lid open until the fire is established. Set the temperature to 380F and preheat, lid closed, for 10 to 15 minutes.
6. Arrange your patties on a grill and cook for 4 minutes per side.
7. Ready! Sprinkle with lemon juice and serve immediately.

Servings: 6

Cooking Times

Inactive Time: 30 minutes

Total Time: 35 minutes

Nutrition Facts

Serving size: 1/6 of a recipe (7 ounces)

Percent daily values based on the Reference Daily Intake (RDI) for a 2000 calorie diet.

Nutrition information calculated from recipe ingredients.

Amount Per Serving

Calories 432,14

Calories From Fat (69%) 299,35

% Daily Value

Total Fat 32,41g 50%

Saturated Fat 12,89g 64%

Cholesterol 144,4mg 48%

Sodium 116,49mg 5%

Potassium 426,24mg 12%

Total Carbohydrates 3,82g 1%

Fiber 0,56g 2%

Sugar 0,09g

Protein 28,52g 57%

Traditional Greek Meatballs

Ingredients

2 1/2 lbs ground beef

1/2 lb ground pork

2 eggs

1 tbsp almond flour

2 spring onions, chopped

2 tbsp fresh parsley, finely chopped

1 tbsp oregano

1 tsp cumin

1 tsp thyme sprigs (fresh)

1/4 cup olive oil

Salt and pepper to taste

Instructions

1. In a large bowl, combine ground beef and ground pork, with eggs, almond flour, spring onion, parsley, oregano, cumin, oil, salt, pepper.
2. Using your hands, knead the meat mixture until combined well.
3. Wet your hands with water, and then form the meat into small meatballs.
4. Start your pellet grill with the lid open until the fire is established. Set the temperature to 380F and preheat, lid closed, for 10 to 15 minutes.
5. Brush the meatballs with olive oil and arrange on a grill rack.
6. Grill the meatballs for about 8 - 10 minutes, or to taste.
7. Serve hot and enjoy!

Servings: 8

Cooking Times

Total Time: 35 minutes

Nutrition Facts

Serving size: 1/8 of a recipe (7 ounces)

Percent daily values based on the Reference Daily Intake (RDI) for a 2000 calorie diet.

Nutrition information calculated from recipe ingredients.

Amount Per Serving

Calories 434,43

Calories From Fat (74%) 296,63

% Daily Value

Total Fat 43,37g 67%

Saturated Fat 15,35g 77%

Cholesterol 173,22mg 58%

Sodium 133,42mg 6%

Potassium 498,94mg 14%

Total Carbohydrates 1,8g <1%

Fiber 0,49g 2%

Sugar 0,18g

Protein 31,74g 63%

GRILLED SAUSAGES
Bacon Cheeseburger Sausages with Mustard

Ingredients

4 Bacon Cheeseburger Sausages

4 buns

2-3 tbsp yellow mustard

Instructions

1. Start your pellet grill, set the temperature on High and preheat, lid closed, for 10 to 15 minutes.
2. Grill your Bacon Cheeseburger Sausages up with indirect heat for about 25 minutes until they hit an internal temperature of 150F.
3. Place your sausages onto a simple bun and hit them with a line of yellow mustard.
4. Serve.

Servings: 4

Cooking Times

Total Time: 30 minutes

Nutrition Facts

Serving size: 1/4 of a recipe (5 ounces)

Percent daily values based on the Reference Daily Intake (RDI) for a 2000 calorie diet.

Nutrition information calculated from recipe ingredients.

Amount Per Serving

Calories 450,7

Calories From Fat (77%) 345,66

% Daily Value

Total Fat 38,36g 59%

Saturated Fat 13,47g 67%

Cholesterol 89,78mg 30%

Sodium 1000,16mg 42%

Potassium 315,07mg 9%

Total Carbohydrates 7,94g 3%

Fiber 0,66g 3%

Sugar 2,64g

Protein 17,42g 35%

Easy Grilled Chicken Sausages Recipe

Ingredients

1 lb chicken sausage links

4 bread rolls (optional)

For serving

Ketchup, mayonnaise, mustard, salad

Instructions

1. Start your pellet grill, set the temperature on High and preheat, lid closed, for 10 to 15 minutes.
2. Bring your sausages to room temperature before grilling.
3. Don't break or score the sausage casing because that casing is holding in all of the juices and fats you want there.
4. Cut each sausage in several places with a knife.
5. Place the sausages directly on the grate and grill, turning occasionally, about 10 minutes.
6. Serve on the bread rolls with your favorite dressing, salad or vegetables.
7. Enjoy!

Servings: 4

Cooking Times

Total Time: 30 minutes

Nutrition Facts

Serving size: 1/4 of a recipe (5 ounces)

Percent daily values based on the Reference Daily Intake (RDI) for a 2000 calorie diet.

Nutrition information calculated from recipe ingredients.

Amount Per Serving

Calories 433,86

Calories From Fat (63%) 272,79

% Daily Value

Total Fat 30,28g 47%

Saturated Fat 10,69g 53%

Cholesterol 68,95mg 23%

Sodium 869,13mg 36%

Potassium 269,94mg 8%

Total Carbohydrates 21,85g 7%

Fiber 0,9g 4%

Sugar 2,69g

Protein 17,01g 34%

Grilled Hot Italian Sausages with Balsamic Peppers

Ingredients

2 tbsp olive oil

1 onion, cut into slices

1 green bell pepper, cut into slices

2 red bell peppers, cut into slices

2 tsp balsamic vinegar

4 hot Italian sausages

Instructions

1. Start your pellet grill, set the temperature on High and preheat, lid closed, for 10 to 15 minutes.
2. Cut peppers and onions into slices, and drizzle with olive oil.
3. Grill peppers and onions 2 - 3 minutes on each side, or until tender.
4. Transfer peppers and onions to a bowl, discarding wooden picks, and toss with balsamic vinegar.
5. Prick your sausages with a fork and grill from all sides or until golden and just cooked through 10 to 15 minutes (sausages have to be cooked through but still juicy).
6. Cut sausages into slices and mix with peppers and onion mixture.
7. Serve and enjoy!

Servings: 4

Cooking Times

Total Time: 25 minutes

Nutrition Facts

Serving size: 1/4 of a recipe (8 ounces)

Percent daily values based on the Reference Daily Intake (RDI) for a 2000 calorie diet.

Nutrition information calculated from recipe ingredients.

Amount Per Serving

Calories 283,18

Calories From Fat (68%) 191,93

% Daily Value

Total Fat 21,66g 33%

Saturated Fat 4,97g 25%

Cholesterol 59,73mg 20%

Sodium 510,38mg 21%

Potassium 264,26mg 8%

Total Carbohydrates 10,69g 4%

Fiber 2,66g 11%

Sugar 5,61g

Protein 12,66g 25%

Grilled Lemony Sausages

Ingredients

8 sausages, whole

1 lemon sliced

1 lemon juice

Oregano

Instructions

1. Start your pellet grill, set the temperature on High and preheat, lid closed, for 10 to 15 minutes.
2. Prick sausages with a fork from both sides.
3. Place the sausages, whole, and grill until they are cooked evenly on all sides and the internal temperature reaches 165 F.
4. Slice a lemon and grill one minute from both sides.
5. Squeeze the lemon juice over the sausages.
6. Sprinkle with oregano and serve.

Servings: 4

Cooking Times

Total Time: 25 minutes

Nutrition Facts

Serving size: 1/4 of a recipe (5.5 ounces)

Percent daily values based on the Reference Daily Intake (RDI) for a 2000 calorie diet.

Nutrition information calculated from recipe ingredients.

Amount Per Serving

Calories 278,3

Calories From Fat (71%) 197,04

% Daily Value

Total Fat 22,22g 34%

Saturated Fat 6,05g 30%

Cholesterol 90,6mg 30%

Sodium 765,34mg 32%

Potassium 30,45mg <1%

Total Carbohydrates 4,05g 1%

Fiber 0,09g <1%

Sugar 0,74g

Protein 17,21g 34%

Grilled Sausage with Sherry Vinegar Peppers

Ingredients

2 tsp sherry vinegar

2 tbsp honey

1/4 tsp kosher salt

16 ounces smoked sausage

3 red, yellow, and/or orange bell peppers

Instructions

1. Preheat grill to medium-high heat (350° to 400°).
2. Whisk sherry vinegar, honey, and salt in a small bowl.
3. Cut sausages in half lengthwise.
4. Grill sausages and peppers 4 minutes on each side.
5. Remove charred skin from peppers and slice into strips. Cut sausages diagonally into 4-inch pieces.
6. Toss peppers and sausages in honey mixture, and transfer to serving platter.
7. Serve hot.

Servings: 4

Nutrition Facts

Serving size: 1/4 of a recipe (8.5 ounces)

Percent daily values based on the Reference Daily Intake (RDI) for a 2000 calorie diet.

Nutrition information calculated from recipe ingredients.

Amount Per Serving

Calories 429,21

Calories From Fat (69%) 297,32

% Daily Value

Total Fat 32,94g 51%

Saturated Fat 11,12g 56%

Cholesterol 65,83mg 22%

Sodium 1156,28mg 48%

Potassium 440,78mg 13%

Total Carbohydrates 18,11g 6%

Fiber 2,31g 9%

Sugar 13,19g

Protein 14,73g 29%

Grilled Sausages with Pickled Allium

Ingredients

8 garlic cloves, peeled and halved

4 red onions, peeled and thinly sliced

1 red pepper, sliced

1 green pepper, sliced

2 lemon zest (finely grated fresh)

1/2 cup lemon juice (2 lemons)

1 tsp cumin seeds

Kosher salt and cracked black pepper to taste

Water

12 oz cooked sausages (pork, chicken or vegetarian)

Instructions

1. Boil the garlic and onions in lightly salted water for one minute; drain.
2. Place the onions and pepper slices in a bowl with the pepper, cumin, salt, lemon juice, and lemon zest; add just enough water to cover.
3. Refrigerate for about 2 - 3 hours. Drain before serving.
4. Start your pellet grill, set the temperature on High and preheat, lid closed, for 10 to 15 minutes.
5. Place the grates back on the grill in the lower position and grill your sausages, rotating them, for about 15 minutes.
6. The sausages have to be cooked evenly on all sides and the internal temperature has to reach 165 F.
7. Slice the sausages into bite-size pieces and serve them with the garlic/onion mixture.

Servings: 6

Cooking Times

Inactive Time: 3 hours

Total Time: 30 minutes

Nutrition Facts

Serving size: 1/6 of a recipe (10 ounces)

Percent daily values based on the Reference Daily Intake (RDI) for a 2000 calorie diet.

Nutrition information calculated from recipe ingredients.

Amount Per Serving

Calories 266,51

Calories From Fat (51%) 135,62

% Daily Value

Total Fat 15,31g 24%

Saturated Fat 4,1g 21%

Cholesterol 60,4mg 20%

Sodium 516,44mg 22%

Potassium 240,49mg 7%

Total Carbohydrates 21,33g 7%

Fiber 4,79g 19%

Sugar 2,16g

Protein 13,77g 28%

Grilled Vienna Sausages-New Potatoes & Snow Peas Skewers

Ingredients

8 new potatoes

16 snow peas

8 Vienna sausages

8 skewers (if you're using bamboo skewers, soak them in water for 30 minutes before grilling)

Ketchup

Instructions

1. Wash the potatoes thoroughly, and wash the sugar snap peas and cut them.
2. Halve the sausages across, and cut from both sides in an X shape.
3. Start the pellet grill to pre-heat at 300 degrees.
4. Layer the sausage, snap peas and one new potato onto each skewer.
5. Put skewers directly on the grill grate and cook for about 5 minutes. Flip skewers over, and grill for an additional 5 minutes.
6. Serve hot with ketchup.

Servings: 4

Cooking Times

Total Time: 25 minutes

Nutrition Facts

Serving size: 1/4 of a recipe (9 ounces)

Percent daily values based on the Reference Daily Intake (RDI) for a 2000 calorie diet.

Nutrition information calculated from recipe ingredients.

Amount Per Serving

Calories 130,72

Calories From Fat (45%) 58,29

% Daily Value

Total Fat 6,48g 10%

Saturated Fat 2,33g 12%

Cholesterol 27,84mg 9%

Sodium 315,52mg 13%

Potassium 304,32mg 9%

Total Carbohydrates 11,1g 4%

Fiber 3,54g 14%

Sugar 5,44g

Protein 7,17g 14%

Grilled Spicy Sausages with Mustard-Caper Sauce

Ingredients

2 lbs of spicy sausages

For mustard sauce

1/3 cup of Dijon mustard

1 cup yogurt

3 tbsp wine vinegar

1 tbsp chopped caper

Coarse pepper black

Instructions

1. Prick sausages all over with a fork.
2. Place the sausages on the grill (place the grates back on the grill in the lower position) and cook on all sides for 10 -12 minutes.
3. Transfer the sausages on parchment paper.
4. Stir all ingredients for the sauce and serve in a bowl next to sausages.

Servings: 6

Cooking Times

Total Time: 20 minutes

Nutrition Facts

Serving size: 1/6 of a recipe (7.5 ounces)

Percent daily values based on the Reference Daily Intake (RDI) for a 2000 calorie diet.

Nutrition information calculated from recipe ingredients.

Amount Per Serving

Calories 337,53

Calories From Fat (71%) 240,54

% Daily Value

Total Fat 27,17g 42%

Saturated Fat 7,28g 36%

Cholesterol 108,72mg 36%

Sodium 1127,55mg 47%

Potassium 25,41mg <1%

Total Carbohydrates 3,78g 1%

Fiber 0,4g 2%

Sugar 0,01g

Protein 21,18g 42%

Grilled Wrapped Bacon Sausages with Mustard Marinade

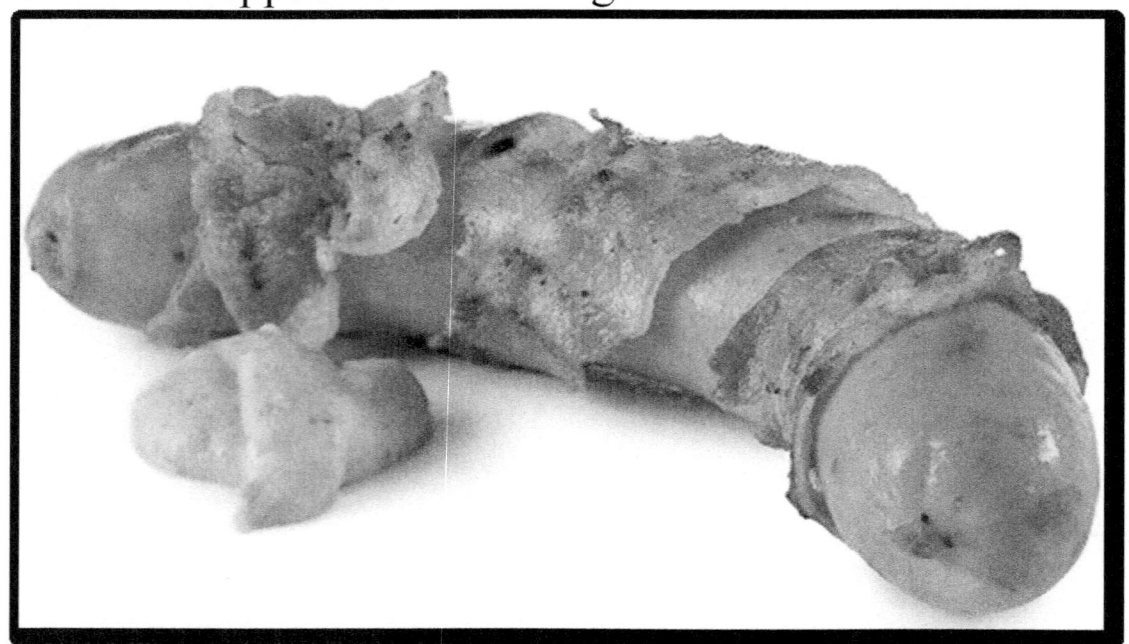

Ingredients

4 tbsp tarragon mustard

2 tsp corn oil

2 tbsp beer

Pepper from the grinder

1/2 tsp sugar

4 sausages

4 slices of bacon

Instructions

1. Place your sausages in a large deep plate.
2. Mix mustard, oil, pepper, and sugar in a small bowl.
3. Pour the mustard mixture over the sausages and refrigerate overnight.
4. The next day, remove the sausages from marinade and wrap every sausage with a slice of bacon.
5. Start your pellet grill, set the temperature on High and preheat, lid closed, for 10 to 15 minutes.
6. Place wrapped sausages on the grill and cook for 15 minutes, rotating them, until they are cooked evenly on all sides.
7. Serve hot.

Servings: 4

Cooking Times

Total Time: 30 minutes

Nutrition Facts

Serving size: 1/4 of a recipe (5 ounces)

Percent daily values based on the Reference Daily Intake (RDI) for a 2000 calorie diet.

Nutrition information calculated from recipe ingredients.

Amount Per Serving

Calories 389,75

Calories From Fat (79%) 309,12

% Daily Value

Total Fat 34,64g 53%

Saturated Fat 10g 50%

Cholesterol 85,57mg 29%

Sodium 1009,07mg 42%

Potassium 100,55mg 3%

Total Carbohydrates 3,33g 1%

Fiber 0,4g 2%

Sugar 0,52g

Protein 16,42g 33%

Smoked Sausages with Mustard and Ketchup

Ingredients

8 mild Italian sausages

1 tsp fresh basil chopped

8 buns

Dijon Mustard

Ketchup, for serving

Instructions

1. Start your pellet grill on SMOKE with the lid open until the fire is established. Set the temperature to 250F and preheat, lid closed, for 10 to 15 minutes.
2. Place the sausages and close the lid. Smoke the sausages about 30-35 minutes.
3. Bump to 325 to finish them off.
4. Transfer sausages in a plate and serve with grilled buns, mustard, and Ketchup.
5. Enjoy!

Servings: 8

Cooking Times

Total Time: 50 minutes

Nutrition Facts

Serving size: 1/8 of a recipe (5 ounces)

Percent daily values based on the Reference Daily Intake (RDI) for a 2000 calorie diet.

Nutrition information calculated from recipe ingredients.

Amount Per Serving

Calories 231,15

Calories From Fat (66%) 151,86

% Daily Value

Total Fat 17,09g 26%

Saturated Fat 4,69g 23%

Cholesterol 63,63mg 21%

Sodium 545,52mg 23%

Potassium 13,98mg <1%

Total Carbohydrates 7,92g 3%

Fiber 0,28g 1%

Sugar 2,54g

Protein 12,09g 24%

GRILLED FISH/SEAFOOD
Grilled Calamari with Mustard Oregano and Parsley Sauce

Ingredients

8 Calamari, cleaned

2 cups of milk

SAUCE

4 tsp of sweet mustard

Juice from 2 lemons

1/2 cup of olive oil

2 tbsp fresh oregano, finely chopped

Pepper, ground

1/2 bunch of parsley, finely chopped

Instructions

1. Clean calamari well and cut into slices.
2. Place calamari in a large metal bow, cover and marinate with milk overnight.
3. The next day, remove calamari from the milk and drain well on paper towel.
4. Grease the fish lightly with olive oil.
5. In a bowl, combine mustard and the juice from the two lemons.
6. Beat lightly and pour the olive oil very slowly; stir until all the ingredients are combined well.
7. Add the oregano and pepper and stir well.
8. Start the pellet grill and set the temperature to moderate; preheat, lid closed, for 10 to 15 minutes.
9. Place the calamari on the grill and cook for 2-3 minutes per side or until it has a bit of char and remove from the grill.
10. Transfer calamari to serving platter and pour them over with mustard sauce and chopped parsley.

Servings: 6

Cooking Times

Total Time: 35 minutes

Nutrition Facts

Serving size: 1/6 of a recipe (9 ounces)

Percent daily values based on the Reference Daily Intake (RDI) for a 2000 calorie diet.

Nutrition information calculated from recipe ingredients.

Amount Per Serving

Calories 212,28

Calories From Fat (82%) 174,78

% Daily Value

Total Fat 19,75g 30%

Saturated Fat 3,54g 18%

Cholesterol 6,51mg 2%

Sodium 57,18mg 2%

Potassium 161,03mg 5%

Total Carbohydrates 7,22g 2%

Fiber 0,75g 3%

Sugar 5,49g

Protein 2,94g 6%

Grilled Cuttlefish with Spinach and Pine Nuts Salad

Ingredients

1/2 cup of olive oil

1 tbsp of lemon juice

1 tsp oregano

Pinch of salt

8 large cuttlefish, cleaned

Spinach, pine nuts, olive oil and vinegar for serving

Instructions

1. Prepare marinade with olive oil, lemon juice, oregano and a pinch of salt pepper (be careful, cuttlefish do not need too much salt).
2. Place the cuttlefish in the marinade, tossing to cover evenly.
3. Cover and marinate for about 1 hour.
4. Remove the cuttlefish from marinade and pat dry them on paper towel.
5. Start the pellet grill, and set the temperature to HIGH and preheat, lid closed, for 10 to 15 minutes.
6. Grill the cuttlefish just 3 - 4 minutes on each side.
7. Serve hot with spinach, pine nuts, olive oil, and vinegar.

Servings: 6

Cooking Times

Inactive Time: 1 hour

Total Time: 30 minutes

Nutrition Facts

Serving size: 1/6 of a recipe (8 ounces)

Percent daily values based on the Reference Daily Intake (RDI) for a 2000 calorie diet.

Nutrition information calculated from recipe ingredients.

Amount Per Serving

Calories 299,34

Calories From Fat (57%) 170,81

% Daily Value

Total Fat 19,31g 30%

Saturated Fat 2,71g 14%

Cholesterol 186,67mg 62%

Sodium 646,75mg 27%

Potassium 780,37mg 22%

Total Carbohydrates 2,84g <1%

Fiber 0,79g 3%

Sugar 0,21g

Protein 28,04g 56%

Grilled Dijon Lemon Catfish Fillets

Ingredients

1/2 cup olive oil

Juice of 4 lemons

2 tbsp Dijon mustard

1/2 tsp salt

1 tsp paprika

Fresh rosemary chopped

4 (6- to 8-oz.) catfish fillets, 1/2-inch thick

Instructions

1. Set the temperature to Medium and preheat, lid closed, for 10 to 15 minutes.
2. Whisk the olive oil, lemon juice, mustard, salt, paprika and chopped rosemary in a bowl.
3. Brush one side of each fish fillet with half of the olive oil-lemon mixture; season with salt and pepper to taste.
4. Grill fillets, covered, 4 to 5 minutes; turn fillets and brush with remaining olive oil-lemon mixture.
5. Grill 4 to 5 minutes more (do not cover).
6. Remove fish fillets to a serving platter, sprinkle with rosemary and serve.

Servings: 6

Cooking Times

Total Time: 20 minutes

Nutrition Facts

Serving size: 1/6 of a recipe (6 ounces)

Percent daily values based on the Reference Daily Intake (RDI) for a 2000 calorie diet.

Nutrition information calculated from recipe ingredients.

Amount Per Serving

Calories 298,76

Calories From Fat (73%) 219,08

% Daily Value

Total Fat 24,66g 38%

Saturated Fat 3,91g 20%

Cholesterol 58,3mg 19%

Sodium 361,28mg 15%

Potassium 376,18mg 11%

Total Carbohydrates 3,25g 1%

Fiber 0,39g 2%

Sugar 1,03g

Protein 16,57g 33%

Grilled Halibut Fillets in Chili Rosemary Marinade

Ingredients

1 cup of virgin olive oil

2 large red chili peppers, chopped

2 cloves garlic, cut into quarters

1 bay leaf

1 twig of rosemary

2 lemons

4 tbsp of white vinegar

4 halibut fillets

Instructions

1. In a large container, mix olive oil, chopped red chili, garlic, bay leaf, rosemary, lemon juice and white vinegar.
2. Submerge halibut fillets and toss to combine well.
3. Cover and marinate in the refrigerator for several hours or overnight.
4. Remove anchovies from marinade and par dry on paper towels for 30 minutes.
5. Start the pellet grill, set the temperature to MEDIUM and preheat, lid closed, for 10 to 15 minutes.
6. Grill the anchovies, skin side down for about 10 minutes, or until the flesh of the fish becomes white (thinner cuts and fillets can cook in as little time as 6 minutes).
7. Turn once during cooking to avoid having the halibut fall apart.
8. Transfer to a large serving platter, pour a little lemon juice over the fish, sprinkle with rosemary and serve.

Servings: 6

Cooking Times

Total Time: 55 minutes

Nutrition Facts

Serving size: 1/6 of a recipe (12 ounces)

Percent daily values based on the Reference Daily Intake (RDI) for a 2000 calorie diet.

Nutrition information calculated from recipe ingredients.

Amount Per Serving

Calories 259,03

Calories From Fat (13%) 33,13

% Daily Value

Total Fat 3,75g 6%

Saturated Fat 0,81g 4%

Cholesterol 133,28mg 44%

Sodium 186,45mg 8%

Potassium 1261,09mg 36%

Total Carbohydrates 5,09g 2%

Fiber 1,85g 7%

Sugar 0,2g

Protein 51,02g 102%

Grilled Lobster with Lemon Butter and Parsley

Ingredients

1 lobster (or more)

1/2 cup fresh butter

2 lemons juice (freshly squeezed)

2 tbsp parsley

Salt and freshly ground pepper to taste

Instructions

1. Use a pot large enough large to hold the lobsters and fill water and salt. Bring to boil and put in lobster. Boil for 4 - 5 minutes.
2. Remove lobster to the working surface.
3. Pull the body to the base of the head and divide the head.
4. Firmly hold the body, with the abdomen upward, and with a sharp knife cut it along in the middle.
5. Start your pellet grill with the lid open until the fire is established (4 to 5 minutes). Set the temperature to 350 degrees F and preheat, lid closed, for 10 to 15 minutes.
6. Melt the butter and beat it with a lemon juice, parsley, salt, and pepper. Spread butter mixture over lobster and put directly on a grill grate.
7. Grill lobsters cut side down about 7 - 8 minutes until the shells are bright in color (also, depends on its size).
8. Turn the lobster over and brush with butter mixture. Grill for another 4 - 5 minutes.
9. Serve hot sprinkled with lemon butter and parsley finely chopped.

Servings: 4

Cooking Times

Total Time: 40 minutes

Nutrition Facts

Serving size: 1/4 of a recipe (10 ounces)

Percent daily values based on the Reference Daily Intake (RDI) for a 2000 calorie diet.

Nutrition information calculated from recipe ingredients.

Amount Per Serving

Calories 385,27

Calories From Fat (57%) 218,36

% Daily Value

Total Fat 24,8g 38%

Saturated Fat 15g 75%

Cholesterol 349,04mg 116%

Sodium 963,84mg 40%

Potassium 501,39mg 14%

Total Carbohydrates 2,18g <1%

Fiber 0,15g <1%

Sugar 0,78g

Protein 37,87g 76%

Grilled Salmon Skewers with French Antilles Sauce

Ingredients

1/2 cup olive oil

1 lime (juice and zest)

1 cup coriander leaves, finely chopped

2 lbs of fresh salmon in thick slices

3 cloves garlic, melted

3 ripe tomatoes, in cubes

5 fresh onions, finely chopped

1/2 cayenne pepper

Salt

Instructions

1. In a deep dish, mix the oil with lime juice and lime zest and half a coriander.
2. Cut the salmon into thick cubes and submerge in marinade; refrigerate for 30 minutes.
3. In a separate bowl, mix the rest of the ingredients and make this exotic sauce, which comes from the French Antilles.
4. Start your pellet grill with the temperature on MEDIUM and preheat, lid closed, for 10 to 15 minutes.
5. Thread the fish on skewers.
6. Grill salmon skewers for 10 - 12 minutes from all sides.
7. Serve hot with French Antilles Sauce.

Servings: 8

Cooking Times

Total Time: 1 hour

Nutrition Facts

Serving size: 1/8 of a recipe (13 ounces)

Percent daily values based on the Reference Daily Intake (RDI) for a 2000 calorie diet.

Nutrition information calculated from recipe ingredients.

Amount Per Serving

Calories 341,71

Calories From Fat (55%) 186,8

% Daily Value

Total Fat 21g 32%

Saturated Fat 3,04g 15%

Cholesterol 62,37mg 21%

Sodium 296,89mg 12%

Potassium 994,71mg 28%

Total Carbohydrates 14,34g 5%

Fiber 3,04g 12%

Sugar 7,31g

Protein 24,75g 50%

Grilled Salmon with Cilantro Butter

Ingredients

1/2 cup fresh butter, softened

1/4 cup fresh cilantro, finely chopped

1 tsp minced garlic

2 tbsp fresh lime juice

1 tsp coriander seeds, lightly toasted and coarsely ground

1/2 tsp sea salt

1/2 tsp crushed red pepper flakes

4 salmon fillets with the skin on, about 6 oz each

Instructions

1. Whisk a bowl place softened butter, cilantro, garlic, lime juice, coriander seeds, salt and red pepper flakes.
2. Brush every salmon fillet generously with butter mixture. Let the salmon sit at room temperature for 15 minutes.
3. Start the grill on Smoke with the lid open until the fire is established (4 to 5 minutes). Set the temperature to MEDIUM and preheat, lid closed, for 10 to 15 minutes.
4. Grill the salmon steaks uncovered, without touching, about 8 - 10 minutes per side.
5. Serve hot.

Servings: 6

Cooking Times

Cooking Time: 25 minutes

Inactive Time: 1 hour

Total Time: 1 hour and 36 minutes

Nutrition Facts

Serving size: 1/6 of a recipe (5 ounces)

Percent daily values based on the Reference Daily Intake (RDI) for a 2000 calorie diet.

Nutrition information calculated from recipe ingredients.

Amount Per Serving

Calories 390,72

Calories From Fat (79%) 309,27

% Daily Value

Total Fat 35,07g 54%

Saturated Fat 20,36g 102%

Cholesterol 104,27mg 35%

Sodium 1564,84mg 45%

Potassium 197,15mg 6%

Total Carbohydrates 0,61g <1%

Fiber 0,23g <1%

Sugar 0,07g

Protein 18,71g 37%

Grilled Trout in White Wine and Parsley Marinade

Ingredients

1/4 cup olive oil

1 lemon juice

1/2 cup of white wine

2 cloves garlic minced

2 tbsp fresh parsley, finely chopped

1 tsp fresh basil, finely chopped

Salt and freshly ground black pepper to taste

4 trout fish, cleaned

Lemon slices for garnish

Instructions

1. In a large container, stir olive oil, lemon juice, wine, garlic, parsley, basil and salt and freshly ground black pepper to taste.
2. Submerge fish in sauce and toss to combine well.
3. Cover and marinate in refrigerate overnight.
4. When ready to cook, start the pellet grill on Smoke with the lid open for 4 to 5 minutes. Set the temperature to 400 degrees F and preheat, lid closed, for 10 to 15 minutes.
5. Remove the fish from marinade and pat dry on paper towel; reserve marinade.
6. Grill trout for 5 minutes from both sides (be careful not to overcook the fish).
7. Pour fish with marinade and serve hot with lemon slices.

Servings: 4

Cooking Times

Total Time: 45 minutes

Nutrition Facts

Serving size: 1/4 of a recipe (6 ounces)

Percent daily values based on the Reference Daily Intake (RDI) for a 2000 calorie diet.

Nutrition information calculated from recipe ingredients.

Amount Per Serving

Calories 267,44

Calories From Fat (62%) 166,95

% Daily Value

Total Fat 18,79g 29%

Saturated Fat 2,79g 14%

Cholesterol 45,82mg 15%

Sodium 44,56mg 2%

Potassium 347,24mg 10%

Total Carbohydrates 2,57g <1%

Fiber 0,27g 1%

Sugar 0,69g

Protein 16,71g 33%

Perfect Smoked Sardine on Pellet Grill

Ingredients

2 lbs sardines

1/4 cup lemon juice, freshly squeezed

1/4 cup olive oil

Fresh oregano

1 lemon, sliced

3/4 cup olives (green or black), sliced

1 onion, sliced

Lettuce salad for serving

Salt to taste

Instructions

1. Clean the sardines; remove the head and giblets and rinse them under cool water to remove any remaining scales.
2. Salt to taste and sprinkle with fresh oregano.
3. In a bowl, whisk lemon juice, oil olive, oregano, and salt.
4. Submerge your sardines in a large, covered, non-reactive container.
5. Let the sardines marinate in the fridge overnight.
6. Take your sardines out of the marinade, rinse under cold water and pat dry on a paper towel for 1 hour.
7. Start pellet grill on with the lid open for 4-5 minutes. Increase the temperature to 225 and allow to pre-heat, lid closed, for 10 - 15 minutes.
8. Gently smoke sardine for 3 hours to an internal temperature of about 140 degrees.
9. Sprinkle with olive oil and lemon juice and serve.

Servings: 4

Cooking Times

Total Time: 3 hours and 30 minutes

Nutrition Facts

Serving size: 1/4 of a recipe (8 ounces)

Percent daily values based on the Reference Daily Intake (RDI) for a 2000 calorie diet.

Nutrition information calculated from recipe ingredients.

Amount Per Serving

Calories 376,9

Calories From Fat (66%) 249,34

% Daily Value

Total Fat 28,08g 43%

Saturated Fat 5,28g 26%

Cholesterol 69,17mg 23%

Sodium 690,64mg 29%

Potassium 464,38mg 13%

Total Carbohydrates 7,08g 2%

Fiber 1,52g 6%

Sugar 2,54g

Protein 24,27g 49%

Stuffed Squid on Pellet Grill

Ingredients

2 lbs. of squid

4 cloves garlic

10 sprigs parsley

4 slices old bread

1/3 cup of milk

Salt and ground white pepper

4 slices of prosciutto

4 slices of cheese

3 tbsp of olive oil

1 lemon

Instructions

1. Wash and clean your squid and pat dry on paper towel.
2. Finely chop parsley and garlic.
3. Cut bread into cubes and soak in milk.
4. Add parsley, garlic, white pepper and salt. Stir well together.
5. Cut the cheese into larger pieces (the pieces should be large enough that they can be pushed through the opening of the squid).
6. Mix the cheese with prosciutto slices and stir well together with remaining ingredients.
7. Use your fingers to open the bag pack of squid and pushed the mixture inside. At the end add some more bread.
8. Close the openings with toothpicks.
9. Start your pellet grill on Smoke with the lid open for 5 minutes.
10. Set the temperature to the highest setting and preheat, lid closed, for 10-15 minutes.
11. Grill squid for 3 - 4 minutes being careful not to burn the squid. Serve hot.

Servings: 8

Cooking Times

Total Time: 30 minutes

Nutrition Facts

Serving size: 1/8 of a recipe (7 ounces)

Percent daily values based on the Reference Daily Intake (RDI) for a 2000 calorie diet.

Nutrition information calculated from recipe ingredients.

Amount Per Serving

Calories 296,23

Calories From Fat (41%) 122,82

% Daily Value

Total Fat 13,89g 21%

Saturated Fat 5,18g 26%

Cholesterol 288,12mg 96%

Sodium 612,96mg 26%

Potassium 390,53mg 11%

Total Carbohydrates 13,14g 4%

Fiber 0,97g 4%

Sugar 1,26g

Protein 29,13g 58%

GRILLED VEGETABLES
Basic Grilled Garlic Eggplant

Ingredients

2 lb eggplant, sliced into rounds

1 lemon juice

1/2 cup extra-virgin olive oil; more as needed

4 cloves garlic, minced

Kosher salt

Fresh parsley for garnish

Instructions

1. Choose large eggplants for this recipe with a smooth and even surface.
2. After washing, remove ends of the eggplant, and cut into thick slices.
3. Place the eggplant slices in a colander, sprinkle with salt and lemon juice and let rest for 20 minutes.
4. Start the pellet grill to pre-heat at 160 degrees.
5. In a large bowl, whisk the olive oil, minced garlic and a pinch of salt.
6. Pour the olive oil mixture over the eggplant slices.
7. Layer the eggplant slices directly on the grill grate in a single layer, and grill for 15 minutes, turning once with a spatula.
8. Sprinkle with parsley and serve hot.

Servings: 6

Cooking Times

Total Time: 35 minutes

Nutrition Facts

Serving size: 1/6 of a recipe (6.5 ounces)

Percent daily values based on the Reference Daily Intake (RDI) for a 2000 calorie diet.

Nutrition information calculated from recipe ingredients.

Amount Per Serving

Calories 41,44

Calories From Fat (6%) 2,65

% Daily Value

Total Fat 0,32g <1%

Saturated Fat 0,06g <1%

Cholesterol 0mg 0%

Sodium 50,46mg 2%

Potassium 365,93mg 10%

Total Carbohydrates 9,96g 3%

Fiber 5,21g 21%

Sugar 3,82g

Protein 1,69g 3%

Grilled Artichokes with Garlic Parsley Sauce

Ingredients

8 artichokes medium

1/4 cup of extra virgin olive oil

4 cloves of garlic minced

A few sprigs of parsley, finely chopped

1 tbsp of lemon juice

Salt

Lemon for garnish

Instructions

1. Pull off the outermost leaves of artichokes until you get down to the lighter, yellow leaves.
2. Using a serrated knife, cut off the top third or so of the artichoke; trim the very bottom of the stem.
3. Use a teaspoon to remove the fibrous 'choke' buried in the center. Discard.
4. Bring a large pot of water to a boil, and cook the artichokes for about 15 minutes.
5. Remove artichokes to a colander.
6. Whisk together the olive oil, garlic, parsley, lemon juice and salt in a bowl.
7. Start your pellet grill, lid open, until the fire is established (4-5 minutes). Increase the temperature to 350F and allow the grill to preheat, lid closed, for 10 - 15 minutes.
8. Pour the garlic/olive oil mixture over the artichokes.
9. Place artichokes on a grill rack and cook for 15 minutes or until deep golden brown.
10. Transfer artichokes on a serving platter, drizzle with olive oil and serve with lemon.

Servings: 6

Cooking Times

Total Time: 55 minutes

Nutrition Facts

Serving size: 1/6 of a recipe (7 ounces)

Percent daily values based on the Reference Daily Intake (RDI) for a 2000 calorie diet.

Nutrition information calculated from recipe ingredients.

Amount Per Serving

Calories 83,82

Calories From Fat (3%) 2,3

% Daily Value

Total Fat 0,27g <1%

Saturated Fat 0,06g <1%

Cholesterol 0mg 0%

Sodium 209,34mg 9%

Potassium 643,1mg 18%

Total Carbohydrates 18,78g 6%

Fiber 9,27g 37%

Sugar 1,78g

Protein 5,72g 11%

Grilled Asparagus with Garlic and Oregano

Ingredients

1 lb fresh asparagus

1/3 cup olive oil

3 cloves garlic, minced

1 lemon zest + juice

1 tbsp dry oregano

1 tsp cayenne pepper

Salt and ground pepper

Fresh thyme chopped, only leaves

Instructions

1. Clean the asparagus by cutting the hard place on its base (it is like wood) and peel off from the waist and down.
2. Place asparagus in a large container.
3. Combine the olive oil, garlic, lemon juice and zest, oregano, cayenne pepper, salt, pepper and thyme in a bowl.
4. Pour the mixture over asparagus.
5. Start the pellet grill on Smoke with the lid open until the fire is established (4 to 5 minutes). Set the temperature to 280°F and preheat, lid closed, for 10 to 15 minutes.
6. Grill the asparagus over medium heat, with the lid closed, until browned in spots but not charred, 6 to 8 minutes, turning occasionally.
7. Serve hot.

Servings: 4

Cooking Times

Total Time: 30 minutes

Nutrition Facts

Serving size: 1/4 of a recipe (4 ounces)

Percent daily values based on the Reference Daily Intake (RDI) for a 2000 calorie diet.

Nutrition information calculated from recipe ingredients.

Amount Per Serving

Calories 179,21

Calories From Fat (90%) 160,44

% Daily Value

Total Fat 18,16g 28%

Saturated Fat 2,54g 13%

Cholesterol 0mg 0%

Sodium 2,4mg <1%

Potassium 160,98mg 5%

Total Carbohydrates 4,18g 1%

Fiber 1,96g 8%

Sugar 1,34g

Protein 1,73g 3%

Grilled Balsamic-Honey Glazed Sweet Onions

Ingredients

2 lb sweet onions (such as Vidalia, Texas Sweet, Walla Walla, Maui)

1/4 cup olive oil

1 cup balsamic vinegar

1/4 cup organic honey

1/4 cup Dijon mustard

1 Tbsp chopped fresh thyme leaves

1/2 tsp crushed pink peppercorns (optional)

1/2 tsp kosher salt; more to taste

Instructions

1. Peel and trim the onions.
2. Cut them crosswise into 1/2-inch-thick slices.
3. Insert a toothpick horizontally halfway into each slice to hold the onion rings together. Transfer the onions to a dish.
4. In a large container, whisk together the olive oil, balsamic vinegar, honey, Dijon mustard, chopped thyme, pink peppercorns and salt and pepper to taste.
5. Pour the balsamic mixture over the onions evenly.
6. Start your pellet grill on Smoke with the lid open until the fire is established. Set the temperature to High (400°F) and preheat, lid closed (10 to 15 minutes).
7. Place the onion on the grill and cook for 10 minutes.
8. After the onion has cooked, transfer to a serving plate and remove toothpicks.
9. Serve hot.

Servings: 6

Cooking Times

Total Time: 35 minutes

Nutrition Facts

Serving size: 1/6 of a recipe (8.5 ounces)

Percent daily values based on the Reference Daily Intake (RDI) for a 2000 calorie diet.

Nutrition information calculated from recipe ingredients.

Amount Per Serving

Calories 139,48

Calories From Fat (2%) 3,34

% Daily Value

Total Fat 0,41g <1%

Saturated Fat 0,03g <1%

Cholesterol 0mg 0%

Sodium 86,68mg 4%

Potassium 266,16mg 8%

Total Carbohydrates 32,25g 11%

Fiber 1,93g 8%

Sugar 26,34g

Protein 1,89g 4%

Smoked Potatoes with Herbs on Pellet Grill

Ingredients

2 lbs potatoes

1/4 cup olive oil

1 shallot chopped

1 tbsp fresh oregano, finely sliced

Finely chopped rosemary

Salt and ground black pepper to taste

Instructions

1. Wash the potatoes and pat dry on kitchen paper towel.
2. Cut the potatoes lengthwise into slices or wedges. Place the potatoes in a large container.
3. Start your pellet grill with the lid open until the fire is established (4 to 5 minutes).
4. Whisk the olive oil, chopped shallot, oregano, rosemary and salt and pepper in a bowl.
5. Brush the potatoes generously all over with olive oil-herbs mixture and place on a grill rack.
6. Cover grill and smoke the potatoes for 1 - 1 hour and 15 minutes without turning.
7. Taste, adjust salt and serve hot.

Servings: 6

Cooking Times

Total Time: 1 hour and 30 minutes

Nutrition Facts

Serving size: 1/6 of a recipe (8 ounces)

Percent daily values based on the Reference Daily Intake (RDI) for a 2000 calorie diet.

Nutrition information calculated from recipe ingredients.

Amount Per Serving

Calories 245,49

Calories From Fat (33%) 81,52

% Daily Value

Total Fat 9,23g 14%

Saturated Fat 1,3g 7%

Cholesterol 0mg 0%

Sodium 17,36mg <1%

Potassium 866,53mg 25%

Total Carbohydrates 38,02g 13%

Fiber 3,65g 15%

Sugar 1,21g

Protein 4,77g 10%

GRILLED RED MEAT
Grilled Goat Skewers with Lemony Herbed Marinade

Ingredients

8 cloves garlic (minced)

2 tsp sweet paprika

2 tsp ground cumin

1 tsp ground chili

1/4 cup olive oil

1/4 cup white vinegar

1 tsp fresh basil, finely chopped

1 tsp fresh mint, finely chopped

Kosher salt to taste

1 lemon juice (freshly squeezed)

2 tsp dried oregano

3 lbs. goat chops, cut into large pieces

Instructions

1. Crush a garlic and give a rough chop.
2. Press garlic with the tines of a fork.
3. Scrape off the fork and press the clove again in the other direction. Repeat the process several times.
4. Mix garlic with sweet paprika, cumin, chili, olive oil, vinegar, salt, basil, mint, fresh lemon juice and dried oregano in a large bowl.
5. Add the goat meat in a marinade and toss to combine well.
6. Cover with plastic wrap and refrigerate several hours or overnight.
7. Set the temperature to 450F (or High) and preheat, lid closed, for 10 to 15 minutes.
8. Remove from fridge 1/2 hour before grilling. Pat dry meet on a kitchen paper towel. Thread the meat cubes onto the skewers.
9. Put skewers directly on grill grate and grill for 5 - 6 minutes from each side, turning occasionally, until browned well.
10. If using an instant-read thermometer look for:

Medium Rare - 145°F

Medium - 160°F

Well Done – 170°F

11. Serve the skewers with the reserved sauce on the side.

Servings: 6

Cooking Times

Inactive Time: 8 hours

Total Time: 25 minutes

Nutrition Facts

Serving size: 1/6 of a recipe (10 ounces)

Percent daily values based on the Reference Daily Intake (RDI) for a 2000 calorie diet.

Nutrition information calculated from recipe ingredients.

Amount Per Serving

Calories 366,45

Calories From Fat (36%) 133,72

% Daily Value

Total Fat 15,01g 23%

Saturated Fat 3,05g 15%

Cholesterol 142,5mg 48%

Sodium 207,7mg 9%

Potassium 1026,77mg 29%

Total Carbohydrates 3,44g 1%

Fiber 0,53g 2%

Sugar 0,33g

Protein 52,03g 104%

Grilled Greek Herb Marinated Lamb Skewers

Ingredients

Marinade

1/3 cup olive oil

2 red onions, roughly chopped

2 cloves of garlic, crushed

Juice of 1 lemon

1/2 tsp cumin (optional)

1 tsp dried Greek oregano

1 tsp fresh thyme, chopped

Salt and freshly ground pepper

Meat

2 lbs lamb legs cut into chunks

10 metal or wooden skewers

Instructions

1. Cut the meat into chunks and set aside (refrigerate).
2. Prepare the marinade: in a large bowl, whisk together onions, garlic, lemon juice, cumin, oregano, thyme and salt and fresh ground black pepper.
3. Submerge meat and toss to coat. Cover the bowl with plastic wrap, and refrigerate overnight.
4. Remove the meat from the bowl and pat dry on paper towel. Reserve some marinade for brushing.
5. Start the pellet grill to pre-heat at 450 F degrees.
6. Thread the meat on metal or wooden skewers.
7. Grill for 4 to 6 minutes per side, or until done to your liking. Serve hot.

Servings: 6

Cooking Times

Total Time: 25 minutes

Nutrition Facts

Serving size: 1/6 of a recipe (8 ounces)

Percent daily values based on the Reference Daily Intake (RDI) for a 2000 calorie diet.

Nutrition information calculated from recipe ingredients.

Amount Per Serving

Calories 428,87

Calories From Fat (68%) 291,3

% Daily Value

Total Fat 32,55g 50%

Saturated Fat 10,45g 52%

Cholesterol 101,3mg 34%

Sodium 88,21mg 4%

Potassium 413,94mg 12%

Total Carbohydrates 4,4g 1%

Fiber 0,81g 3%

Sugar 0,27g

Protein 28,66g 57%

Grilled Lamb Chops with Herbed Brown Sugar Marinade

Ingredients

4 lamb chops

1/4 cup brown sugar

1 tsp garlic powder

2 tsp ground ginger

2 tsp dried tarragon

1 tsp ground cinnamon

Salt and ground black pepper to taste

Instructions

1. Mix brown sugar, ginger, tarragon, cinnamon, pepper, garlic powder, and salt in a bowl. Rub lamb chops with the brown sugar mix, and place in a deep.
2. Cover, and refrigerate for 2 hours (preferably overnight).
3. Set the temperature to HIGH (450F) and preheat, lid closed, for 10 to 15 minutes.
4. Remove the lamb chops from marinade and place directly on grill grate.
5. Grill for 10 to 15 minutes per side (135F internal temperature for medium-rare).
6. Serve hot with your favorite vegetables or salad.

Servings: 4

Cooking Times

Inactive Time: 2 hours

Total Time: 20 minutes

Nutrition Facts

Serving size: 1/4 of a recipe (7 ounces)

Percent daily values based on the Reference Daily Intake (RDI) for a 2000 calorie diet.

Nutrition information calculated from recipe ingredients.

Amount Per Serving

Calories 369,83

Calories From Fat (52%) 193,98

% Daily Value

Total Fat 21,51g 33%

Saturated Fat 10,3g 52%

Cholesterol 98,34mg 33%

Sodium 92,94mg 4%

Potassium 519,31mg 15%

Total Carbohydrates 15,24g 5%

Fiber 0,53g 2%

Sugar 13,39g

Protein 27,7g 55%

Grilled Orange-Turmeric Lamb Skewers

Ingredients

1 lb boneless lamb meat, boneless cut into 1/2" cubes

Marinade

2 tbsp orange juice

1 cup plain low-fat yogurt

1/4 tsp ground ginger

1/2 tsp turmeric

1/2 tsp ground cumin

1 tbsp ground coriander

1/2 tsp salt

Skewers

Instructions

1. Cut boneless lamb meat into 1/2" cubes.
2. Whisk together all ingredients from the list in a large bowl.
3. Add the lamb meat cubes to the bowl, and stir to coat with the marinade evenly. Cover and refrigerate overnight.
4. Remove the bowl with marinated lamb 15 - 20 minutes before grilling.
5. Start the pellet grill to pre-heat with the lid open until the fire is established; about 5 minutes. Set the temperature to High and preheat, lid closed, for 10 to 15 minutes.
6. Remove the meat from the marinade, pat lightly with paper towels to dry. Place meat evenly on the skewers.
7. Perfectly grilled lamb chops skewers will take about 4 - 5 minutes on each side.
8. Serve hot.

Servings: 4

Cooking Times

Total Time: 20 minutes

Nutrition Facts

Serving size: 1/4 of a recipe (7 ounces)

Percent daily values based on the Reference Daily Intake (RDI) for a 2000 calorie diet.

Nutrition information calculated from recipe ingredients.

Amount Per Serving

Calories 171,46

Calories From Fat (20%) 34,7

% Daily Value

Total Fat 3,89g 6%

Saturated Fat 1,44g 7%

Cholesterol 68,31mg 23%

Sodium 427,62mg 18%

Potassium 623,47mg 18%

Total Carbohydrates 6,12g 2%

Fiber 0,63g 3%

Sugar 4,98g

Protein 26,86g 54%

Grilled Rabbit with Wine and Rosemary Marinade

Ingredients

1 rabbit cut into pieces

For marinade

3 cloves of garlic, mashed

1 1/2 tsp rosemary

1 cup of white wine, dry

1/2 cup olive oil

1 tbsp white vinegar

1 tsp mustard

1/2 tsp cumin

Salt and ground pepper to taste

Instructions

1. In a large bowl, whisk all marinade ingredients from the list.
2. Place the rabbit meat in marinade and toss to combine well.
3. Cover with plastic wrap and refrigerate for several hours (preferably overnight).
4. Remove meat from marinade and pat dry on a paper towel.
5. Set the temperature to High and preheat your pellet grill, lid closed, for 10 to 15 minutes.
6. Place the rabbit pieces directly on grill rack.
7. Grill for about 12 to 15 minutes per side.
8. An instant-read meat thermometer inserted into the thickest part of a piece should read at least 160 degrees.
9. The rabbit meat is ready when no longer pink inside and the juices run clear.
10. Serve hot.

Servings: 6

Cooking Times

Total Time: 40 minutes

Nutrition Facts

Serving size: 1/6 of a recipe (8.5 ounces)

Percent daily values based on the Reference Daily Intake (RDI) for a 2000 calorie diet.

Nutrition information calculated from recipe ingredients.

Amount Per Serving

Calories 420,6

Calories From Fat (58%) 243,75

% Daily Value

Total Fat 27,37g 42%

Saturated Fat 5,28g 26%

Cholesterol 95mg 32%

Sodium 80,59mg 3%

Potassium 587,75mg 17%

Total Carbohydrates 1,48g <1%

Fiber 0,17g <1%

Sugar 0,39g

Protein 33,53g 67%

GRILLED GAME
Grilled Wild Boar Steaks with Blueberry Sauce

Ingredients

4 large steaks of wild boar

For the marinade

2 glasses dry red wine

Juice from 1 lemon, preferably organic

2 bay leaves

2 tbsp sweet paprika powder

1 cup fresh celery, finely chopped

Salt and black pepper, crushed

1 tsp rosemary fresh or dry

For the sauce

3/4 lbs blueberries

1 tsp brown sugar

Salt and white freshly ground pepper to taste

Instructions

1. Wash and wipe the wild boar steaks.
2. In a large and deep pan, place all the ingredients for the marinade and mix well.
3. Submerge the wild boar steaks in marinade and refrigerate overnight.
4. The next day, drain the wild boar steaks (strain the marinade and set aside) and wipe them well with kitchen towels.
5. Start the pellet grill to pre-heat at 500 degrees, lid closed, for 10 to 15 minutes.
6. Place the steaks on grill and close lid and cook about (5) minutes on each side for medium steak, or 8-10 minutes for large steaks.
7. In the meantime, make a sauce: In a saucepan heat all the ingredients all sauce ingredients and bring to boil over medium heat. Boil for 2 minutes, stirring and remove from the fire.
8. Transfer the sauce to your blender and beat until smooth and creamy.
9. Serve the steaks immediately with the blueberry sauce.

Servings: 6

Cooking Times

Total Time: 40 minutes

Nutrition Facts

Serving size: 1/6 of a recipe (10 ounces)

Percent daily values based on the Reference Daily Intake (RDI) for a 2000 calorie diet.

Nutrition information calculated from recipe ingredients.

Amount Per Serving

Calories 232,65

Calories From Fat (18%) 42,2

% Daily Value

Total Fat 4,69g 7%

Saturated Fat 1,35g 7%

Cholesterol 0mg 0%

Sodium 18,28mg <1%

Potassium 151,04mg 4%

Total Carbohydrates 11,18g 4%

Fiber 1,73g 7%

Sugar 7,22g

Protein 29,3g 59%

Grilled Wild Goose Breast in Beer Marinade

Ingredients

4 goose breasts

2 cups beer of your choice

1 1/2 tsp Worcestershire sauce

1 tsp garlic powder

1/2 tsp paprika

Salt and pepper

Instructions

1. Place the goose breasts in a Ziploc plastic bag.
2. Pour in the beer, Worcestershire sauce, garlic powder, paprika, and salt and pepper. Close the bag and shake to combine all ingredients well.
3. Marinate in refrigerated for 2 hours.
4. Remove the goose meat from marinade and par dry on kitchen towel (reserve the marinade).
5. Preheat a grill for medium heat, about 300 degrees F.
6. Place the goose breasts on the grate. Brush occasionally with the marinade only for the first half an hour.
7. Continue to cook for 10 - 15 minutes longer or until reach an internal temperature of 165 degrees F.
8. Serve hot.

Servings: 4

Cooking Times

Inactive Time: 2 hours

Total Time: 50 minutes

Nutrition Facts

Serving size: 1/4 of a recipe (6 ounces)

Percent daily values based on the Reference Daily Intake (RDI) for a 2000 calorie diet.

Nutrition information calculated from recipe ingredients.

Amount Per Serving

Calories 153,76

Calories From Fat (39%) 59,68

% Daily Value

Total Fat 6,64g 10%

Saturated Fat 2,59g 13%

Cholesterol 77,7mg 26%

Sodium 99,51mg 4%

Potassium 419,3mg 12%

Total Carbohydrates 1,08g <1%

Fiber 0,17g <1%

Sugar 0,24g

Protein 21,21g 42%

Grilled Wild Rabbit with Rosemary and Garlic

Ingredients

1 - 2 wild rabbits (about 2 pounds)

2 clove of garlic, melted

2 tbsp of rosemary dried, crushed

Juice from 1 lemon

1/4 cup olive oil

Salt and freshly ground pepper

Instructions

1. If we use a whole rabbit, cut into portions as follows: cut up a rabbit by removing the front legs, which are not attached to the body by bone.
2. Slide your knife up from underneath, along the ribs, and slice through. Cut the trunk into slices of 4-5 cm thick.
3. In a bowl, mix the garlic, rosemary, oil, salt and pepper, and lemon juice.
4. Brush the rabbit pieces with the garlic-rosemary mixtures.
5. Start the pellet grill to pre-heat to 300 degrees and preheat, lid closed, for 10 to 15 minutes.
6. Lay the rabbit pieces onto grill rack.
7. Grill for about 12 - 15 minutes per side, or until the meat is no longer pink inside.
8. Serve.

Servings: 4

Cooking Times

Total Time: 1 hour and 15 minutes

Nutrition Facts

Serving size: 1/4 of a recipe (9 ounces)

Percent daily values based on the Reference Daily Intake (RDI) for a 2000 calorie diet.

Nutrition information calculated from recipe ingredients.

Amount Per Serving

Calories 384,49

Calories From Fat (44%) 167,59

% Daily Value

Total Fat 18,85g 29%

Saturated Fat 3,46g 17%

Cholesterol 183,71mg 61%

Sodium 114,29mg 5%

Potassium 884,36mg 25%

Total Carbohydrates 1,69g <1%

Fiber 0,2g <1%

Sugar 0,39g

Protein 49,59g 99%

Author Notes

For safety, USDA recommends cooking rabbit to an internal temperature of at least 160 °F.

Smoked Aromatic Pheasant on Pellet Grill

Ingredients

1 large pheasant

3/4 cup fresh butter

1 tsp fresh basil, finely chopped

1 tsp fresh thyme, finely chopped

1 tsp parsley, finely chopped

Salt and ground pepper

1/2 cup white wine

Instructions

1. Wash the pheasant, pat dry with a paper towel, and tie cross its legs.
2. In a small saucepan melt the butter over medium heat.
3. Add the basil, parsley and thyme, wine and salt and pepper; stir well and remove from heat.
4. Brush the pheasant generously with the herbed butter mixtures.
5. Start your pellet grill, and set the temperature to 350F and preheat, lid closed, for 10 to 15 minutes.
6. Smoke the pheasant 3 hours - 5 hours.
7. When the pheasant reaches an internal temperature of 160°F in the thigh meat, take out of the smoker.
8. Chop the pheasant and serve hot.

Servings: 4

Cooking Times

Total Time: 5 hours

Nutrition Facts

Serving size: 1/4 of a recipe (6 ounces)

Percent daily values based on the Reference Daily Intake (RDI) for a 2000 calorie diet.

Nutrition information calculated from recipe ingredients.

Amount Per Serving

Calories 443,64

Calories From Fat (74%) 328,59

% Daily Value

Total Fat 37,31g 57%

Saturated Fat 22,81g 114%

Cholesterol 140,52mg 47%

Sodium 34,68mg 1%

Potassium 249,46mg 7%

Total Carbohydrates 1,2g <1%

Fiber 0,27g 1%

Sugar 0,32g

Protein 21,1g 42%

Stuffed Wild Duck on Pellet Grill

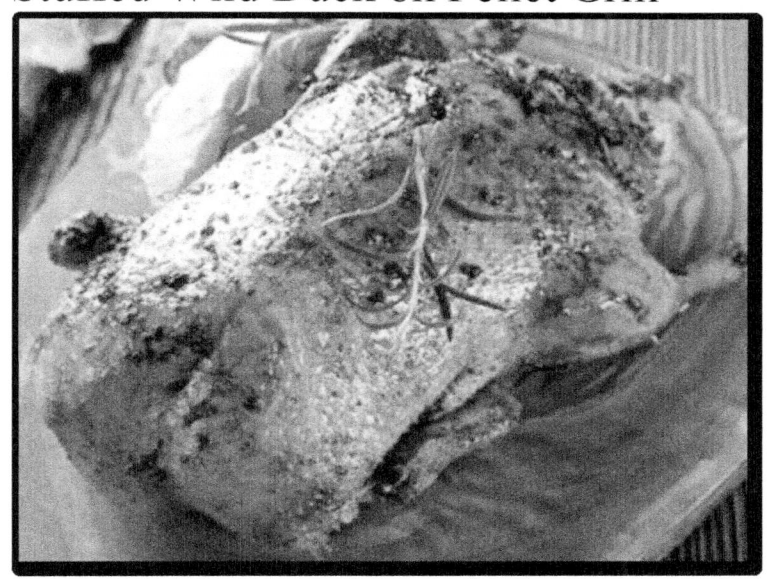

Ingredients

1 wild duck (about 4 pounds), cleaned

1 mushrooms cut into slices

1 tsp fresh parsley, finely chopped

1/2 tsp of thyme

1/4 cup fresh butter

Salt and pepper

Instructions

1. In a bowl, combine mushrooms, parsley, thyme, fresh butter and salt and pepper.
2. Place the mushrooms mixture in the wild duck belly.
3. Start the pellet grill on Smoke with the lid open until the fire is established (4 to 5 minutes).
4. Set the temperature to 350F and preheat, lid closed, for 10 to 15 minutes.
5. Place the duck directly on the grill grate.
6. Cover the grill and cook the duck for 1-1/2 hours.
7. After 1-1/2 hours, drain the juices and fat from the pan and flip the duck, breast side down.
8. Let the duck cool down, pull the twigs and serve.

Servings: 6

Cooking Times

Total Time: 2 hours

Nutrition Facts

Serving size: 1/6 of a recipe (7 ounces)

Percent daily values based on the Reference Daily Intake (RDI) for a 2000 calorie diet.

Nutrition information calculated from recipe ingredients.

Amount Per Serving

Calories 405,09

Calories From Fat (70%) 285,58

% Daily Value

Total Fat 31,91g 49%

Saturated Fat 12,89g 64%

Cholesterol 147,8mg 49%

Sodium 90,6mg 4%

Potassium 410,93mg 12%

Total Carbohydrates 0,19g <1%

Fiber 0,08g <1%

Sugar 0,07g

Protein 27,95g 56%

References

http://www.letstalkbbq.com/index.php?topic=19503.0 (how long do wood pellets last)

http://www.pelletsmoking.com/pellet-smoking-com-lounge-9/question-how-long-pellets-last-6955/ (how many pellets DO)

http://www.chimneysweeponline.com/howood.htm (BTU content of pellets/woods)

http://www.bbq-brethren.com/forum/archive/index.php/t-88739.html (should you use heating pellets for smoking)

www.cookbook.com (grilling recipes)

Printed in Great Britain
by Amazon